THE
SOLICITOR GENERAL'S
STYLE GUIDE
THIRD EDITION

28 U.S.C. 505 – Solicitor General

"The President shall appoint in the
Department of Justice, by and with the
advice and consent of the Senate,
a Solicitor General, learned in the law,
to assist the Attorney General in the
performance of his duties."

"[W]hat the Court concluded was, it was done by the Committee of Style, and the Committee of Style had no authority to
change the substance, and indeed, during that period it was
quite often the case that alternative formulations were used
that had no substantive significance."

– Solicitor General Drew Days
U.S. Term Limits, Inc. v. *Thornton,*
Oral argument, May 22, 1995

THE
SOLICITOR GENERAL'S
STYLE GUIDE

THIRD EDITION

Office of the Solicitor General
United States Department of Justice

Edited and User's Guide by
Jack Metzler

~◊~
interAlias
Washington, D.C.

Suggested citations:

This *Guide* generally:	S.G. Style Guide — (3d ed. 2018).
OSG Citation Manual Rule:	S.G. Citation R. — (3d ed. 2018).
OSG Supplement to the Supreme Court Rules Rule:	S.G. Supp. S.Ct. R — (3d ed. 2018).
OSG Writing Preferences:	S.G. Writing Pref. —, S.G. Style Guide — (3d ed. 2018).

ISBN 978-0-9911163-5-5

Contents

Office of the Solicitor General Style Manual

Appendix

User's Guide to the Third Edition

This Third Edition of Solicitor General's Style Guide reprints, in edited form, the April 2018 version of the Office of the Solicitor General Style Manual, the citation and style manual that the Solicitor General's office (OSG) uses to prepare briefs in the Supreme Court and the federal courts of appeal. The *2018 Update* contains more than 100 changes from the next-most-recent version, which was completed in 2014.[1] Although the changes are too numerous to describe individually, this User's Guide identifies the new and significantly updated material. It also describes some of the more notable changes to OSG's preferences and explains the editorial changes imposed on the *2018 Update*.

1. Structure. The overall structure of the 2018 is largely unchanged. A few general changes are worth noting, however.

a. As before, the "Current versions of Chapters" shows that every "chapter" has been updated; however, OSG may be coming to the realization that the manual is unlikely to be updated one rule at a time—unlike in previous editions, the month and year no longer appears at the bottom of each page.

b. The introduction to the Bluepages has been updated. Specifically, a sentence noting that the Supreme Court Rules do not mandate deviations from the Bluebook, but "experience has often suggested preferred alternative conventions" has been replaced by descriptions of two rules that do mandate some differences. Unfortunately, deleting the part about "preferred alternative conventions" leaves the next sentence, referring back to "those preferred stylistic differences," somewhat adrift.

c. In accordance with Rule 15.1, which mandates that when an author is a government agency, "the smaller department comes before the larger entity," I have changed the order of "United States Department of Justice" and "Office of the Solicitor General" on the cover and title page of the *Guide*.

---

[1] At print time, the 2014 version (but not the *2018 Update*) is available on OSG's website at the following URL: https://www.justice.gov/osg/osg-citation-manual-2014.pdf.

2. New rules.   The 2018 Update contains new entries for eight Bluebook rules:

Rule 1.4	Rule 10.1	Rule 10.2.1(j)	Rule 10.8.1(c)
Rule 15.3	Rule 16.3	Rule 16.9	Rule 18.2

It also contains two new rules (A.4 and A.10) in the OSG Supplement to the Supreme Court Rules, and, in the OSG Writing Preferences, four new typographical preferences (F.2-F.5), and one new "Miscellaneous Preference."

3. New information and examples.   New information or preferences (beyond minor editorial changes) has been added to 31 Bluebook rules, 3 rules in the OSG Supplement to the Supreme Court Rules, and 4 writing preferences

Bluebook Rules:

B4	B7	B7.3.1	Rule 1.2
Rule 1.5	Rule 3.2(a)	Rule 4.1	Rule 5.1
Rule 5.1(a)/(b)	Rule 5.3	Rule 10	Rule 10.2.1(c)
Rule 10.4	Rule 10.6	Rule 10.7	Rule 10.8.1(b)
Rule 10.3.3	Rule 12.3	Rule 12.3.1	Rule 12.3.2
Rule 12.4(a)	Rule 12.9.3	Rule 12.9.5	Rule 13.3
Rule 13.4(a)	Rule 13.5	Rule 14.1	Rule 14.2(a)
Rule 15.10	Rule 21.4	BT1	

OSG Supplement to Supreme Court Rules:

A.1	A.2	D.1

OSG Writing Preferences:

C.1	D.6	D.8	F.1

In addition, twenty-five rules have new examples:

B2	B6	Rule 1.2	Rule 3.1(c)
Rule 3.2(a)	Rule 3.5	Rule 4.1	Rule 5.1
Rule 6.1	Rule 10.1	Rule 10.2.1	Rule 10.5(c)
Rule 10.7	Rule 10.8.1(b)	Rule 10.9	Rule 12.3
Rule 12.3.1(a)	Rule 12.3.1(e)	Rule 12.4(a)	Rule 12.9.5
Rule 13.3	Rule 13.4(a)	Rule 14.1	Rule 15.10
Rule 21.4			

4.   New typography rule.   Although OSG's prior practice was to change underscored text to italics when documents are reproduced an appendix, Rule B1 now states that the text "remains underscored per the original.   To this editor's eye, this is an odd change to make; italics and underscoring are typically understood to mean the same thing.   Underlining originated as a way to indicate the emphasis using a typewriter—it's not necessary for documents prepared using modern word processing software, as Supreme Court Rule 33 requires for appendices.

5.   Attorneys' preferences.   A new sentence has been added to Rule B4:   "It is an attorney's discretion whether to use a short form for cases."   Although seemingly minor, this may have become an issue in OSG, since this point (or a variation of it) has been added no fewer than eleven times in the *2018 Update*.

6.   New abbreviation preference.   Continuing the trend started in the 2014 update—which mandated for the first time that "page" be abbreviated ("p.")—"note" must now be abbreviated "n."

7.   New parenthetical preferences.   Rule 1.5 contains new preferences on the order of parentheticals, including a change: in parentheticals noting that emphasis has been added and something else (for example brackets) has been omitted, the addition comes first. Although not stated specifically, based on the other examples it appears that omissions precede things that were in the original, so the order is (1) additions; (2) omissions; (3) things that stayed the same.

Rule 1.5 also contains new preferences for omitting internal citations and other material, stating that attorneys should use "citation omitted" and not "internal citation omitted."   However, that rule has not been propagated throughout the *2018 Update*; Rule 5.3 still mandates "internal citation omitted," and, confusingly, contains examples using both forms.[2]

8.   New preference for citing the Federal Register.   Rule 3.2(a) previously forbade citing the first page of a document in addition to a

---

[2] Sadly, the *2018 Update* does not endorse the use of "(cleaned up)," a new parenthetical intended to make quotations that contain a quotation easier to read.   See Jack Metzler, *Cleaning Up Quotations*, 18 J. Appellate Practice & Process 143 (2017).

pin cite when citing the Federal Register. It now *requires* that the first page be included. The rule suggests that the change was prompted by making the citation consistent with the table of authorities, which "will only have the citation including the first page on which a document begins."

9. One space or two space? The *2018 Update* continues OSG's silence on whether to use one or two spaces after a period, but two new preferences strongly suggest that the Office uses two. First, Rule 5.3 now mandates two spaces both before and after an ellipsis.[3] Second, Miscellaneous Typographical Preference 3 (Misc. Writing Pref. F.3) states that two spaces *should* be used after colon, but gives attorneys discretion to use one space instead. Thus, it appears highly likely that the oversize spaces in OSG briefs likewise contain two spaces.[4] However, the discretion afforded attorneys to use a single space after a colon suggests there may yet be hope that OSG will one day permit attorneys to do the same after a period. Stay tuned.

10. Repeated cert. denials. If you have ever wonder how to write a paragraph explaining that the Supreme Court has repeatedly denied certiorari on the same issue, you're in luck—Rule 10.7 now provides an example. The rule also includes a new and extremely complicated set of examples on how to cite multiple successive denials of certiorari in the same case, depending on the year of the decisions and whether they appear in the same or different volumes of the United States Reports.

11. New brief cover preferences. Rule A.1 of the OSG Supplement to the Supreme Court Rules now notes that when agency counsel is listed on the cover of a brief, the columns should be aligned at the bottom if the agency counsel listing is shorter than the DOJ counsel listing. If the list of agency counsel is longer, however, Rule A.2 mandates that attorneys make sure that the Solicitor General's name is higher than anyone listed on the left side of the brief.

Rule A.10 contains new example cover pages for capital cases and information about where to place "Capital Case" on the cover and the

---

[3] Although it tends to take up a lot of space, ellipses throughout the *Guide* now conform to this rule.

[4] This *Guide* continues to use one em space after periods and colons.

Questions Presented page. Although the *2018 Update* prints both of these examples in Courier, the *Guide* conforms to how they would actually appear, with the paid case typeset and the IFP case in Courier.

12. New typographical preferences. In addition to the new preference for the number of spaces after colons, Writing Preferences F.2, F.4, and F.5 contain preferences for avoiding bad line breaks, when to use two dashes versus em dashes, and proper kerning settings.

13. Editorial changes. Sadly, the *2018 Update* appears to have eschewed almost every single edit suggested in the Second Edition of this *Guide*. Accordingly, all of the corrections listed *infra* at pages xiv-xvi have been carried over to this edition. In addition, typos have been corrected minor changes have been made throughout for consistency. In a number of places, *i.e.* has been changed to *e.g.* or vice versa, in accordance with the apparent intent.

One change was not implemented. The example for Rule 15.1 illustrates how to cite the author of a book that has more than one author, but in the *2018 Revision*, the author information in the example was stripped; instead, Professor Keeton is listed parenthetically as the editor. This volume retains the old version so that it will continue to be a relevant example. If you'd like to see the revised example, which is presumably how *Prosser* should be cited, you can find it in the first example for Rule 15.10.

14. Bonus material! Intrepid reader Brendan Kenny, interested in the memorandum from Charles Fried described in OSG Writing Preference D.3, requested a copy from OSG via the Freedom of Information Act. Unfortunately, no responsive documents were found.[5] OSG's response is included as an Appendix to the *Guide*.

15. Acknowledgements. Thanks once again to the dedicated public servants in the Office of the Solicitor General.

---

[5] OSG's failure to locate the memo calls the "see" signal in Writing Preference D.3 into serious doubt.

User's Guide to the Second Edition

The Solicitor General's Style Guide reprints, in edited form, the *Office of the Solicitor General Style Manual*, which, as its name suggests, is the style manual used by that office in preparing briefs to be filed in the Supreme Court and the courts of appeals. When the first edition the *Guide* was published in 2013, the *Manual* had last been updated in June 2007.[1] In April 2014, the Office of the Solicitor General (OSG) issued a substantially updated and revised version of the *Manual* (*2014 Update*); hence, this second edition of the *Guide*.

Although the practices of OSG have changed little in substance, the *2014 Update* reflects a major overhaul of the *Manual*. Not only were many sections rewritten or edited for clarity, the *Manual* was updated to reflect changes in the Bluebook and the Supreme Court Rules. Some of the more notable changes are described below, as are some new features of the *Guide* implemented by the editor.

1. Updated references and structure. For the *2014 Update*, OSG has moved from the 16th edition of the Bluebook (1999) to the 19th edition (2010).[2] Accordingly, Part I of the *Manual*, which is structured to parallel the Bluebook, has been revised to reflect changes between the two volumes. For example, the 16th edition began with a set of Practitioner's Notes,[3] which in the 18th edition were rebranded as the "Bluepages." The *Manual* has been updated accordingly (without changing the color of the pages), with one exception: In the Bluebook, the table that lists abbreviations commonly used in court documents (formerly known as T8; now known as BT1) appears immediately after the Bluepages. The authors of the *Manual* prudently left it with the rest of the tables. In addition, a few rules have changed numbers and others have been eliminated entirely. The *2014 Update* conforms the *Manual* to those changes. The *2014 Update* also removed numerous placeholders for rules that have no corresponding OSG preference.

---

[1] "*Manual*" refers to OSG's version of its style guide. "*Guide*" refers to this edited version.

[2] The Bluebook is now in its 20th edition, published in 2015.

[3] The Bluebook's conceit is that its rules are primarily for law reviews rather than court filings, but the litigators know better.

The *2014 Update* also abandons reliance on the 1984 version of the GPO Style Guide, adopting instead the 2008 version as the fallback for matters not specifically addressed in the *Manual*. See Introduction, *infra* p. 3. The 2008 version of the GPO Style Guide is available through a hyperlink directly to the GPO website (which should work in the electronic edition of the *Guide*). *Ibid.*

2. Rewritten rules and new preferences. With the *2014 Update*, OSG has rewritten many rules for clarity. In general, the rewritten sections evince a preference for the active voice and simpler sentences. For example, Rule 16.2 (regarding citations to works appearing in periodicals) has been sensibly rewritten to require "the author's full name," rather than the unnecessarily complex "the author's last name, preceded by the first and middle names."

In addition, the *Manual* has adopted some new preferences:

a. New (secret?) miscellaneous grammar preference: Use "cite" as a transitive verb, not as a noun. The *Manual* has decided that one cites authorities; one does not cite *to* authorities. Accordingly, the preposition "to" has been excised wherever it followed "cite" as a verb. In addition, "cite" has been eliminated where used as a noun, replaced in nearly every case[4] by "citation." Further complicating matters, "to" *may* be used with the word "citation." Thus, "citation to" an authority is acceptable, but one may not "cite to" an authority. This last complication, however, may be on its way out. In several places, the *2014 Update* replaces the phrase "citation to" with "citation of." *E.g.*, Rule 3.2(a). Stay tuned.

b. Abbreviate "page" in cross-references. Rule 3.5, *infra* p. 27, formerly expressed a preference for spelling out "note" and abbreviating "page" in internal cross-references, but gave attorneys the discretion to spell out "page" if done consistently. That discretion has been eliminated.

c. New italicization preferences. The word "habeas" has apparently "become so incorporated into English usage" that it rates the list of foreign words that require no italicization. See Rule 7(b),

---

[4] The editor converted the few stray appearances of "cite" as a noun to conform with the apparent new edict.

infra p. 41.   No word yet on *corpus*.   Meanwhile, *inter alia* joins the list of terms that OSG will continue to italicize.   *Ibid.*

d.   New abbreviation preferences.   OSG has added "int'l" to the words that the Bluebook recommends should always be abbreviated in case names.   See Rule 6.1, *infra* p. 37; Rule 10.2.1(c), *infra* p. 47. In addition, the *2014 Update* changed the standard abbreviation for "exhibit" from Exh. to Ex. (the latter conforms with Bluebook table BT1).   See, *e.g.*, Rule B7, *infra* p. 8.   One abbreviation preference has been removed: There is no longer a preferred abbreviation for "affirm."

e.   New short-citation preference.   In a rather startling addition, the *2014 Update* mandates, contrary to Bluebook Rule 10.9(a)(i) and (c), that OSG will "formally establish" short forms for cases in a parenthetical even when the short form "adopts the first word or words of a party's name."   Rule 10.9, *infra* p. 64.   The Bluebook rule does not go quite that far; it permits short forms that employ a party name as long as the reference is "unambiguous."   It's possible that OSG has done this all along, but in at least one recent brief checked by the editor, OSG did not use "(*Chevron*)" to introduce *Chevron* as a short form for *Chevron*.   Compare Gov't Br. at 21, *Michigan* v. *EPA*, 135 S. Ct. 2699 (2005) (No. 14-46) (full citation with no parenthetical short citation defined) with *id.* at 23 ("Under *Chevron* * * * ").

f.   The Federalist.   In Rule 15.8(c), *infra* p. 81, the *Manual* expresses a new preference for versions of The Federalist *other than* Clinton Rossiter's edition.   That version "should be disfavored, not simply because it has the wrong title (The Federalist Papers)" but also because it "is not intended to be a scholarly edition" and has "modernized both spelling and punctuation."   *Ibid.*

Setting aside the merits of the preference, OSG should be commended for taking a principled stand in what may be a lost cause. The Court cited the Rossiter edition of The Federalist as recently as the last day of the 2014 Term, in both the majority and dissenting opinions.   See *Arizona State Legis.* v. *Arizona Indep. Redistricting Comm'n*, 135 S. Ct. 2652, 2672 (Ginsburg, J.); *id.* at 2679 (Roberts, C.J., dissenting).   The last citation to Rossiter before that was just two days earlier, in *Obergefell* v. *Hodges*, 135 S. Ct. 2584, 2611 (Roberts, C.J., dissenting).   Indeed, in addition to the Chief and Justice

Ginsburg, Justices Scalia, Kennedy, and Sotomayor all cited Rossiter during the most recent Term. See *Zivotofsky* v. *Kerry*, 135 S. Ct. 2076, 2085 (2015) (Kennedy, J.); *id.* at 2099 (Scalia, J., dissenting); *Perez* v. *Mortgage Bankers Ass'n*, 135 S. Ct. 1199 (2015) (Alito, J., concurring in part); *Wellness Int'l Network, Ltd.* v. *Sharif*, 135 S. Ct. 1932, 1951 (Sotomayor, J.). However, all may not yet be lost. Justices Scalia, Breyer, and Kagan have also cited Jacob E. Cooke's version of The Federalist.[5] See, *e.g.*, *Armstrong* v. *Exceptional Child Ctr.*, 135 S. Ct. 1378, 1383 (2015) (Scalia, J.); *NLRB* v. *Canning*, 134 S. Ct. 2550, 2558 (2014) (Breyer, J.); *Michigan* v. *Bay Mills Indian Cmty.*, 134 S. Ct. 2024 (2014) (Kagan, J.). Notably, Justice Kagan came to the Court directly from OSG, and may have been influenced by its preferences. In addition, Chief Justice Roberts and Justice Alito, both veterans of OSG, might yet be convinced to abandon Rossiter.

    g.   Update to Supplement to Supreme Court Rules. The examples of Supreme Court Brief cover pages now include OSG's email address, as required by Supreme Court Rule 33.1(f).

    h. New typography preference: The newly added OSG Writing Preference F, the very last entry in the *Manual*, instructs that a "hair space" should be inserted after a lowercase "f" and "j," when those letters are followed by an apostrophe, quotation mark, parenthesis, or bracket. An example of how this looks can be seen in the sentence you just read. To insert such a space in Microsoft Word, either type 2009 and then press Alt-X, or hold down the Alt key and type 8201 on the numeric keypad.

    3.   Typography. As noted in the introduction to the first edition of the *Guide, infra* p. xvii, the 2007 version of the *Manual* was typeset entirely in Courier, using underlining, boldface, and sometimes all-caps for emphasis. For the *2014 Update*, the *Manual* has moved to Century Expanded (the font in which that OSG's briefs are set) for its rules, but has retained Courier for the examples. In addition, the *2014 Update* continues to eschew italics in favor of underlining and sometimes boldface for emphasis.

As in the first edition of the *Guide*, text in Courier has been reset in a proportional-width serif font; however, the second edition has

---

[5] On this issue, Scalia appears to be the swing Justice.

been set in Century Expanded rather than Century Schoolbook. The second edition is also follows the first in its use of italics for emphasis, largely replacing OSG's underlining and boldface. There is one exception to this: in a some places the *2014 Update* uses boldface to draw attention to the relevant part of an example. The *Guide* has incorporated this feature.

The second edition of the *Guide* also employs, for the first time, an "em space" (i.e., a special space that is the width of a capital "M") between sentences and after a colon. This represents a middle-course in the number-of-spaces-after-a-sentence war. An em space is just one space, but it is significantly wider than an ordinary space. After painstaking research, the editor settled on the em space after concluding that the United States Reports uses the em space in this manner, and appears to have done so for a long long time.

In addition, where the *Manual* includes explanatory information about an example citation in brackets immediately following the example, the *Guide* now retains the brackets rather than changing them to parentheses. The conversion to parenthesis was based on the explanatory information resembling a parenthetical, in that it explains the example. On further reflection, OSG's examples more closely resemble a block quotation; brackets are thus appropriate for the explanatory material because that material is not part of the citation; and thus not part of the "quotation."

4. New features of the *Guide*. The second edition has been fully hyperlinked. Thus, in the electronic version of the *Guide*, the table of contents should reliably link to the appropriate section of the *Manual*, and internal cross-references likewise should take the reader to the cross-referenced section. The print version continues to use page numbers as an alternative to hyperlinks, both for the table of contents and for internal cross-references.

5. Editorial changes. The *2014 Update* fixed many, but not all of the errors corrected in the first edition of the *Guide*. For example, the *Manual*'s multiple misspellings of *Shelley* v. *Kraemer* (*e.g.*, Rule 10.5, *infra* p. 52) persist in the *2014 Update*, but have been corrected in the *Guide*.

In accordance with the advice of the introduction, *infra* p. 3, the following list of edits is provided as a set of recommendations for the use of the Director of the Legal Research and Publications Unit in updating the *Manual*.

Rule	Change
B1	This rule purported to describe the "only exception" to the rule that OSG does not italicize the *v.* in a case name, but now lists three exceptions. Changed to "only exceptions are" and changed "or" to "and" before the last exception.
B2	Changed first example, "As we stated earlier (Pet. Br. 3)" to "Pet. 3" because OSG would never refer to its own brief as "Pet. Br." If it were the government's brief it would be Gov't Br. or U.S. Br.; if it were the government's petition it would be "Pet." See Rule B7, *infra* p. 8.
B5	Changed short citation to § 2, 103 Stat. *at* 1299, in accordance with Bluebook rule 12.10.
B7	Changed one sentence in the first paragraph to avoid awkward construction (A, B, and C, as well as D).
	Added second "a" for parallel construction: "When citing a table in a document, *a* regulation, or legislative material, use the abbreviation 'Tbl.'"
	Removed redundant phrase in "When introducing page references * * * do not use "at" *to introduce page references* * * * ."
B7.3.3	Added "capitalized and" to this sentence, regarding the titles of Supreme Court documents: "The titles are, however, *capitalized and* abbreviated when used in citation sentences." This retains the substance of the rule, which appears to have been inadvertently lost in the *2014 Update*.
1.6(a)	Edited one sentence to make it parallel and to remove an awkward construction (without this edit, the sentence retains the disfavored phrase "cite to"). Also removed extraneous parentheses around the final paragraph of this rule.

3.2(a)   Removed quotation marks around examples in second parenthetical (to conform to the first parenthetical). Also, in the paragraph beginning "Also," removed brackets around "s" in "citations."

Corrected cross-reference (ironically, to the section on cross-references) from Rule. 3.6 to Rule 3.5.

3.3(b)   Removed addition of "subsections" in second paragraph, which would otherwise have read, "We will not drop digits in citing multiple * * * subsections[.] * * * We will, however, continue to drop repetitive digits and letters when citing a number of *subsections*."

3.4   Corrected cross-reference from Rule 3.3(a) to Rule 3.2(a).

4.2(a)   Removed "to" from "cited to generally" and changed "short cite" to "short citation," to conform to other revisions.

5.1   Changed "single and double quotations" to "single and double quotation **marks**."

Changed references to *Chevron U.S.A. Inc. v. NRDC*, 467 U.S. 837 (1984) to be consistent with one another, and with a recent OSG brief in which *Chevron* was cited. See Gov't Br., *Michigan* v. *EPA*, 135 S. Ct. 2699 (2005) (No. 14-46). Interestingly, OSG's citation for *Chevron* differs from the Supreme Court's in that OSG lists the respondent in that case as "NRDC" whereas the Court spells out "Natural Resources Defense Council, Inc." Compare *ibid.* with, *e.g.*, *Michigan* v. *EPA*, 135 S. Ct. at 2706-2707.

6.1   Removed quotation marks around each item in the list of words that are always abbreviated to be consistent with similar changes elsewhere in the *2014 Update*. Similar changes were made to Rule 10.2.1(c).

6.2(a) and (b)   Moved sentence regarding commas in four-digit numbers so it would not separate the rule for five-digit numbers from its exception.

6.2(c)   Altered to indicate that emphasis was added to the Rule's quotation of Bluebook rule 12.4(d), to conform to the treatment of the same quotation (with the same emphasis addition) in Rule 3.3.

7   Removed quotation marks around foreign phrases that will *not* be italicized, to conform to the rest of the rule.

8   Moved the link to the GPO Style Manual to its own line for aesthetic reasons. Removed redundant phrase in table entry for ship names: "for the names **for the names** of ships and aircraft."

10.5(c)   Much of this rule is reproduced as if it were an example. It has been reformatted for clarity.

6. Attachment 1. As described in the user's guide to the first edition, "Attachment 1" to the *Manual* presented somewhat of a mystery during the editing of that volume. The *Manual* describes Attachment 1 as having been supplied by the Supreme Court's Reporter of Decisions, but (in the 2007 version of the *Manual*) it contained some apparently incomplete or incorrect citations, including one that did not appear to support the sentence preceding it. For that citation, the editor guessed that *Estelle* v. *Gamble*, 429 U.S. 97 (1976), was the intended reference.

Since the first edition was published, the editor has discovered that the source of Attachment 1 is section 10.4 of the style guide used by the Reporter of Decisions in preparing Supreme Court opinions for publication and—perhaps more importantly—that the editor's *Estelle* guess was correct. The *2014 Update* includes an edited version of Attachment 1, but that version has been discarded in favor of a more recent (and more accurate) version of section 10.4 of the Reporter's style guide, which also contains a new and interesting discussion of the opinions in *Planned Parenthood of Southeastern Pa.* v. *Casey*, 505 U.S. 833 (1992).

7. Acknowledgements. The editor expresses thanks once again to the dedicated public servants in the Office of the Solicitor General.

User's Guide to the First Edition

Consider yourself lucky. You are holding in your hands the *Office of the Solicitor General Style Manual*, a resource previously available only to the handful of attorneys and paralegals working in the Office of the Solicitor General (OSG). If you picked this book up, you probably know that the Solicitor General represents the United States in the Supreme Court, which makes OSG the most frequent—and often the most skilled—practitioner before the Court.

The *Style Manual* has not previously been released to the public. Google Books tantalizingly lists a 24-page volume titled *Style and Citation Manual for Office of the Solicitor General: Supreme Court Briefs*, authored by the United States Department of Justice in 1941, but that book is not for sale anywhere, nor does any library the editor could find appear to own a copy. So the information you hold has until now been rare.

It is also valuable. The briefs filed by the Solicitor General are often held up as models for creating appellate briefs. And you now have a nuts-and-bolts guide to creating briefs the way they do in the Office of the Solicitor General. However, while this manual may help you *cite* like the Solicitor General, it cannot help you *write* like the Solicitor General. For tips on writing good appellate briefs, get *Making Your Case: The Art of Persuading Judges*, which resulted from the collaboration of Justice Scalia and legal-writing guru Bryan Garner. That volume also contains helpful pointers to other legal writing and style resources.

Despite its rarity and value, however, the *Style Manual* must be taken in the context in which it was created. Though it was written by OSG, it was not written for the Supreme Court to read, nor for the public. It was intended as an internal guide to ensure that OSG's briefs remain consistent in specific ways despite the passage of time and changes in personnel. Considering the importance of OSG's regular work, it is not surprising that the authors of the *Style Manual* prioritized the substance of the information it contains over its form. Accordingly, the *Manual* does not reflect the careful attention to detail and consistency that usually characterizes a brief publicly filed by the Solicitor General. In this regard the *Style Manual* implicitly implores the reader to do as it *says*, not as it *does*.

Yet the primary purpose of *this* volume (as opposed to the *Style Manual*'s internal purposes within OSG) is to serve as a reference for those who admire and wish to emulate briefs filed by OSG. Because typos and inconsistencies tend to distract the reader, the *Manual* has been edited with the goal of maximizing its usability without changing its content. In general the edits are intended to make the *Style Manual* consistent with (a) the *Style Manual* itself; (b) the U.S. Government Printing Office Style Manual;[1] and (c) the editor's understanding of ordinary English usage.[2] The notes below describe the changes and reflect the editor's observations about parts of the *Manual* that were not changed.

1. Title of the *Manual*. Perhaps the most audacious change made in this volume was to change its title from the "Office of the Solicitor General Citation Manual" to the "Office of the Solicitor General Style Manual."[3] The original title page dubs the work the "Citation" manual, but the contents pages refer only to part I by that name, and call the overall work the "Style" manual. The overall work includes not only the *OSG Citation Manual* (in part I), but also the *OSG Supplement to the Supreme Court Rules* (part II) and the *OSG Writing Preferences* (part III).

The organization suggested by the contents pages—titling the overall work the *OSG Style Manual* and part I the *OSG Citation Manual*—is the most consistent with other references in the book. Part I of the *Manual* is preceded by a title page dubbing it (rather than the overall work) the "Office of the Solicitor General Citation Manual," and its introduction explains that the "Citation Manual" is "designed to showcase only the ways in which the OSG citation style differs from the [Bluebook]" and is "organized to mirror the format of the Bluebook." That is true only of part I; parts II and III cover other topics. The introduction also refers to previous versions of the "OSG Style Manual," which were formatted differently, *ibid.*, implying that the prior versions may have incorporated the non-citation preferences described in parts II and III of the current version.

---

[1] Though the *Manual* prefers the 1984 version of the *GPO Style Manual*, this volume employed the 2008 version.

[2] This last category is, alas, the least reliable.

[3] This book has yet another title, "The Solicitor General's Style Guide," to distinguish it from the *Style Manual*.

However, it should be noted that the *Manual* also refers to itself as the OSG "Citation Style Manual," and the "Office Rules of Style." The former reference appears to refer to the citation guidelines in part I, and the latter appears to refer to the writing preferences in part III. Despite these anomalies, the editor believes this volume will be more useful and less confusing to the reader if the title of the overall work matches the table of contents.

2. Typography and formatting. The 2007 version of the *Style Manual* reproduced here is, substantively, the current version in use by OSG as of September 2013. The OSG version, however, is formatted using Courier font with justified margins, on 8.5 x 11 inch paper, stapled in the upper left-hand corner. This is similar to the requirements for documents submitted to the Supreme Court under its Rule 33.2. This version of the *Style Manual*, on the other hand, was prepared for publication in tradition of (though not in strict compliance with) the requirements for documents submitted in "booklet format" under Rule 33.1. Accordingly, the *Manual* has been re-typeset using 11-point Century Schoolbook with 10-point footnotes. See Supreme Court R. 33.1(b). Although the Court has required that briefs use 12-point type since 2007, *ibid.*, the editor is comfortable with 11-point type (which the Court required before 2007) on the basis that we do have costs to contend with here.

The pagination style has been retained; *i.e.*, we have used Roman numerals to number introductory pages and Arabic numbers for the remaining pages, but page breaks have not been retained. The table of contents reflects the pagination of this volume.

Italics have been retained in part I (*OSG Citation Manual*) and III (*OSG Writing Preferences*). Underlining has been replaced with italics in those parts. Boldface type has been retained in headings and replaced with italics where it appears to have been used for emphasis. Type in all caps has also been retained, reluctantly. Where boldface, underlining, and all caps appear together, for example: **INTRODUCTION** on page 1, the underlining has been omitted. As the Seventh Circuit puts it: "Underlined, all-caps, boldface text is almost illegible." U.S. Court of Appeals for the Seventh Circuit, *Practitioner's Handbook for Appeals* 115 (2012). Of course, the Seventh Circuit also advises, "Use proportionally spaced type," and "Do not justify monospaced type." *Id.* at 114. The authors of the *Style Manual* went a different way than those suggestions too.

In part II (*OSG Supplement to the Supreme Court Rules*), the *Style Manual* uses boldface to indicate emphasis. This has been changed to italics. In addition, to match OSG's practice regarding the covers of booklet-format briefs filed in the Supreme Court, party and attorney names in all caps have been changed to small caps in the examples[4] and brief titles have been rendered in boldface.[5]

3. Typographic errors and stylistic changes. Apparent typos have been corrected. For example, two references to the "Blue Book" have been changed to "Bluebook." References to Roman numerals and Arabic numbers have been capitalized. Parentheses, brackets, and quotation marks have been added or deleted to make a matched set or to remove strays according to the editor's best guess of the authors' intent. Other corrections include misspelled words, subject-verb agreement, errors in basic citation form, and the occasional dropped word.[6]

---

[4] OSG's e-mail address, SupremeCtBriefs@usdoj.gov, has not been added to the examples, though it is now required by Supreme Court Rule 33.1(f) and thus appears on OSG's briefs.

[5] This presented a problem for the first example in OSG Supplement to Supreme Court Rule A(5), "BRIEF FOR THE SECURITIES AND EXCHANGE COMMISSION AS AMICUS CURIAE." The rule requires that the name of the agency be on the first line of the title, but in 11-point Century Schoolbook the line breaks before "COMMISSION." The editor could not find an example of a brief filed on behalf of that agency as amicus curiae where the agency (rather than the United States) was listed in the title of the brief. Accordingly, though an imperfect solution, the font was reduced to 10 points in order to accommodate the agency name on a single line.

[6] The editor struggled with several corrections. For example, the *Style Manual* uses *Shelley* v. *Kraemer* as a fictional example case with a docket number indicating it was filed in 1983, though a case by that name was decided in 1948. See 334 U.S. 1. But the *Style Manual* spells *Shelley* without the second "e." With no indication the misspelling was an intentional fictionalization, it was corrected as distracting. The same holds for the dropped final "t" in the last name of former Secretary of the Interior Bruce Babbitt. In Rule 13.5, on the other hand, the editor could not determine the authors' intent, and thus left the obvious typo, "except that di the following examples" for the reader's interpretation.

The editor has also imposed, with some hesitancy, certain stylistic changes on the *Manual.*[7] For example, commas and periods have been moved inside the quotation marks and serial commas have been added to be consistent with the GPO Style Manual.

Approximately 250 typographic and stylistic edits were made to the *Style Manual.*

4. Citation corrections.   Attachment 1 to the *OSG Citation Manual* provides guidance on referring to plurality opinions in Supreme Court cases.   According to note 3, *infra* p. 54, this guidance was supplied by the Supreme Court's Reporter of Decisions.   Oddly, given that provenance, the guidance used a nonstandard form for several citations; those have been corrected. One citation, "492 U.S. 10, 11. 7-8," did not appear to relate to the sentence that preceded it.   This was changed to *Estelle* v. *Gamble*, 429 U.S. 97, 102 (1976), which appears in the cited volume of the United States Reports and supports the preceding sentence; however, the editor cannot be sure this was the intended reference.

5. Editorial change.   In part II, OSG Writing Preference D(1), the phonetic spellings were edited for clarity and consistency.

6.   Acknowledgments.   The editor extends thanks to the Office of the Solicitor General and its dedicated public servants, who are worthy role models for excellence in lawyering.

The editor hopes you enjoy using the *Office of the Solicitor General Style Manual* as much as he has enjoyed editing it.

---

[7] These changes have been made for consistency, and every effort was made to ensure that there was no underlying rationale for the inconsistency.   Yet the editor cannot guarantee accuracy in this regard.   Indeed, without the *Style Manual*, one would be hard pressed to reverse engineer many of the rules it contains from OSG's filings in the Supreme Court.

United States Department of Justice

OFFICE OF THE SOLICITOR GENERAL STYLE MANUAL

Revised February 2018

OFFICE OF THE SOLICITOR GENERAL STYLE MANUAL

CURRENT VERSIONS OF CHAPTERS

Revised February 2018

I.   OSG Citation Manual:

I

II. OSG Supplement to the Supreme Court Rules:

III. Miscellaneous OSG Writing Preferences:

OFFICE OF THE SOLICITOR GENERAL
STYLE MANUAL

TABLE OF CONTENTS

Revised February 2018

I.   OSG Citation Manual:

Bluepages*

General Rules of Citation and Style

1.   Structure and Use of Citations

Constitutions, Statutes, and Legislative, Administrative, and Executive Materials

Tables

OFFICE OF THE SOLICITOR GENERAL CITATION MANUAL

Revised February 2018

OFFICE OF THE SOLICITOR GENERAL
CITATION MANUAL

Revised February 2018

INTRODUCTION

The *Office of the Solicitor General Citation Manual* is designed to showcase only the ways in which the OSG citation style differs from the *19th Edition* of the Bluebook, or where a Bluebook Rule needs emphasizing due to common errors. Where a rule is not listed below, it can be assumed that the Bluebook rule governs. Where a rule is listed below, the rule is designed to *supplement* the Bluebook rule, not replace it.

For additional guidance on punctuation, capitalization, compounding, and other matters of style, you may wish to consult the *U.S. Government Printing Office Style Manual* (2008), available at: http://www.gpo.gov/fdsys/pkg/GPO-STYLEMANUAL-2008/pdf/GPO-STYLEMANUAL-2008.pdf.

Recognizing that the Bluebook is the primary source for citation style, this manual is organized to mirror the format of the Bluebook. Users of this manual should consult the Bluebook first, and then check the same rule in this manual.

This manual will be periodically updated. A list of the current versions of all chapters is included on pages I-II; users of this manual should ensure that their copy contains the most recent versions of chapters. To suggest changes to this manual or to obtain the most recent version of specific chapters, please contact the Director of the Research and Publications Unit.

B   Bluepages

The Bluepages in the Bluebook are generally good guidelines for the preparation of briefs for the Supreme Court. Supreme Court Rule 33.1(b) provides that quotations over 50 words be indented; OSG practice is to indent only on the left side. In addition, Supreme Court Rule 34.5 states that "[a]ll references to a provision of federal statutory law should ordinarily be cited to the United States Code, if the provision has been codified therein. * * * Additional or alternative citations should be provided only if there is a particular reason why those citations are relevant or necessary to the argument." This OSG Style Manual sets forth those preferred stylistic differences.

B1   Typeface Conventions

While Rule B1's statement that there are typically only two typefaces in court documents is generally correct, OSG alters this rule for appendices, which ordinarily will duplicate the typeface used in the original document. For example, if a court of appeals opinion uses large and small capitals (*e.g.*, in citing a book title), the OSG appendix will also use large and small capitals.

There are a few exceptions to this rule, but most involve the cover and signature pages of briefs and the captions of court opinions reproduced in appendices. See *OSG Supplement to the Supreme Court Rules*, below, for examples for cover and signature pages using large and small capitals.

B1 also states that *italics* or underscoring are used interchangeably depending on the format of the document. When an IFP brief is filed under Supreme Court Rule 33.2, underscoring is the appropriate typeface convention. In any document prepared under Supreme Court Rule 33.1, italics is the appropriate typeface convention. For appendices, text (including headings) that is underscored in the original document remains underscored per the original in the printed appendix.

Case Names

The "v." in case names is *not* italicized. The only exceptions to this rule are that the "v." or "versus" *is* italicized in a quote, in the captions of briefs, and in court opinions included in appendices.

Introductory Signals

Introductory signals are neither underscored nor italicized, with "*e.g.*" as the sole exception to this rule.

Explanatory Phrases Introducing Prior or Subsequent History

Explanatory phrases introducing prior or subsequent history are neither underscored nor italicized.

B2   Citation Sentences and Clauses

Citations may be set off from text by the use of commas or parentheses. While a parenthetical may either precede or follow text containing assertions for which the citation is provided, a comma is ordinarily used only when the text containing assertions for which a citation is provided precedes the citation. Where a comma or a pair of parentheses is used to set off citations from text in one clause of a sentence, text in other clauses of the same sentence should ordinarily be set off by the same form.

There is no requirement that citations precede indented quotations. Instead, OSG style permits, but does not require, a citation to follow an indented quotation (appearing at the left margin of the line immediately following the quotation).

Often, authors will refer to court filings within the text, eliminating the need to repeat in the citation the information that is already contained in the text. See the following examples:

Petitioner contends (Pet. 3) * * * .

Petitioner contends (Br. 3) * * * .

As we stated earlier (Pet. Br. 3) * * * .

As we stated in our petition (at 3) * * * .

The amicus maintains (ACLU Br. 8) * * * .

The ACLU maintains (Amicus Br. 8) * * * .

We believe (Gov't Br. 9) * * * .

In our initial brief (at 9) * * * .

B3   **Introductory Signals**

Despite the Bluebook's preference for italicizing, the only signal we italicize is *"e.g."*

When used as a verb in a textual sentence, a signal normally abbreviated must be spelled out; "cf." becomes "compare," and *"e.g."* becomes "for example."

B4   **Sources and Authorities: Cases**

For short citation forms, clarity and ease in locating a full citation are the governing principles. There are instances in which a full citation is required or preferred. It is an attorney's discretion whether to use a short form for cases. A full citation must be used the first time a source is cited in the brief. If a source is cited for the first time in a footnote, however, the source must be cited in full *both* in the footnote and where it first appears in the text.[1]

Although attorney preference and space constraints may dictate otherwise, it is preferred that a source be cited in full the first time it is cited in the statement of interest, statement,

---

[1] There is one narrow exception to this rule. An attorney may have cited in a footnote a source with an unusually lengthy citation and does not want to repeat the full citation the first time it is used in the text (*e.g.*, a case with a lengthy case history). In those cases, these examples can be followed:

See *Jones* v. *United States*, *supra* p. 2 n.4, 697 F.2d at 1197.

See *Hearings*, *supra* p. 5 n.7, at 16.

summary of argument, and argument/discussion sections of the brief. If a short form is used, it is the attorney's discretion as to whether it appears with the full citation for the first time in the statement, summary of argument, or argument/discussion sections. Subsequent citations within the same section may take a short form.

If a short form is used, the location of the short form would appear after the citation and before any subsequent history. For example:

> *Voest-Alpine Trading USA Corp.* v. *Bank of China*, 142 F.3d 3887, 890 (5th Cir.) (*Voest-Alpine*), cert. denied, 525 U.S. 1041 (1988).

"*Id.* at" and "*ibid.*" are not to be used when there is an intervening citation (see Rule 4.1).

B4.2 Short Form Citation

A short form for cases that includes both parties' names, rather than only one, may be used, but such form should be used consistently throughout the brief.

B5 Sources and Authorities: Statutes, Rules, and Regulations

The Internal Revenue Code will be cited with references to 26 U.S.C. (not "I.R.C."). Do not include section symbols (§) in citations to Internal Revenue Code sections in the brief; however, include section symbols (§) with sections of the Internal Revenue Code in the table of authorities.

Citations to the United States Code and the Code of Federal Regulations may use the form "*ibid.*," but not "*id.* at" or any of the short forms listed in Bluebook Rule 12.10; unless "*ibid.*" is appropriate, these sources must be cited in full each time. Citations to the Statutes at Large, state statutory codes, and state session laws may take a short form. For example:

The Support for Eastern European Democracy Act (SEED) of 1989, Pub. L. No. 101-179, 103 Stat. 1298, was enacted on November 28, 1989. It required the United States to "implement * * * a concerted Program of Support for East European Democracy" designed to "provide cost-effective assistance to those countries of Eastern Europe that have taken substantial steps toward institutionalizing political democracy." § 2, 103 Stat. 1299.

Searches of committed persons charged with an offense may be "for the purpose of discovering any money or property he may have." **Mo. Ann. Stat. § 542.300 (West 1987).** Any search "shall be conducted in a reasonable manner." *Id.* § 542.291.

B6   Sources and Authorities: Constitutions

U.S. Const. Art. I § 8, Cl. 5.

U.S. Const. Amend. V.

B7   Sources And Authorities: Court and Litigation Documents

Citations to court filings (unlike textual references to court filings) are abbreviated. Thus: "J.S." (jurisdictional statement), "Mot. to Affirm" (motion to affirm), "Pet." (petition), "Br. in Opp." (brief in opposition), and so forth. Use "Pet. Br." and "Resp. Br." to refer to briefs for nongovernment parties, "Gov't Br." to refer to briefs on behalf of federal officials or agencies, and "U.S. Br." to refer to briefs for the United States. Spell out "Appellant's," "Appellee's," and "Reply," as well as other identifying adjectives that would create confusion if abbreviated.

In general, any pleading filed in the court of appeals can be cited by adding "C.A." to the appropriate abbreviation (*e.g.*, Jones C.A. Br., Resp. C.A. Br., Pet. C.A. Br., etc.). To avoid confusion when citing briefs for the United States filed in courts of appeals, avoid the form "U.S. C.A. Br." and use instead "Gov't C.A. Br." No footnoted explanations are necessary for any of these conventions.

The first time Administrative Record or Presentence Investigation Report is cited, the full name needs to be provided followed by (A.R.) or (PSR) whether it is cited textually or as a citation the first time. For example:

The Presentence Investigation Report (PSR) states * * * . PSR ¶ 15.

Presentence Investigation Report (PSR) ¶ 2.

Judgment will be spelled out when appearing alone, but abbreviated when it is used as Summary J.

For common named court documents, *e.g.*, Judgment, Gov't C.A. Br., no date is provided in a parenthetical if there is only one document. If there are, for example, multiple judgments, a date would be provided as: 1/21/15 Judgment, as is done for transcripts. If there are multiple, for example, government court of appeal briefs in multiple dockets, the lower-court case number would be used, *e.g.*, 15-222 Gov't C.A. Br. If there is more than one, for example, government court of appeal brief filed within the same docket, then a date will be used, *e.g.*, 1/21/15 Gov't C.A. Br.

Use "App." to refer to an appendix that is bound together with the document or filing that it accompanies (*e.g.*, Pet. App., J.S. App.). Use "J.A." to refer to the separately bound joint appendix filed in connection with a merits brief in the Supreme Court. Where there is only one appendix or a joint appendix filed in the court of appeals, it is cited "C.A. App." When there is more than one appendix or when there are citations to appendices from the Fifth, Sixth, Ninth, or Eleventh Circuits, follow these examples:

Appellant's App.

Appellee's App.

Gov't C.A. App.   [United States appendix or appendix for an agency]

83-1844 C.A. App.   [multiple case number appendix]

Jones C.A. App.   [multiple party appendix]

C.A. E.R.   [Excerpts of Record, Ninth Circuit]

C.A. R.E.   [Record Excerpts, Fifth and Eleventh Circuits]

C.A. ROA.   [Record on Appeal, Fifth and Sixth Circuits]

When a brief contains multiple appendices, do not cite a specific appendix (*e.g.*, J.S. App. A, Pet. App. D) except in unusual circumstances (*e.g.*, when multiple appendices are separately paginated, citations to a specific appendix are necessary).   As long as the appendix pages are consecutively or distinctively numbered, it is accurate and helpful to the reader to cite the page numbers in referring to the various appendices of a particular brief.   Thus:

The court of appeals affirmed.   Pet. App. 1a-45a.

NOT:

The court of appeals affirmed.   Pet. App. A.

BUT for separately paginated appendices:

The court of appeals affirmed.   Pet. App. A1-A45.

Use the form "App., *infra*, 1a-5a" when referring to an appendix *bound together* with the brief in which it is cited.   When the appendix is *separately bound*, use the form "Pet. App." or "App." without "*infra.*"

When citing particular pages in the record or transcript, use the abbreviation "R." or "Tr." The default is to cite a transcript as "Tr.," but an attorney has the discretion to cite it as a "Tr." or as a district court document.   When citing a multivolume record or transcript, include the volume number that appears on the cover page.   The volume number should always be in Arabic numerals.   If there is no volume number, the date can be used in place of the volume number.   When citing a table in a document, a regulation, or legislative material, use the abbreviation "Tbl." Examples:

4 R. 68.

NOT: IV R. 68.

Tbl.

5/15/02 Tr. 322.

[*Note*: The date used is the date of the hearing, not the date in which the document was filed in the court.]

If a short form is created at the attorney's discretion, the location of the short form would be after "5/15/02 Tr." For example:

5/15/02 Tr. (Tr.) 322.

Exhibits are cited as "Ex.," "U.S. Ex.," "GX," "PX," or "DX."

It often will not be sufficient to use one of the above conventions without supplying additional identifying information when citing court filings. Examples of such situations are citations to court documents filed in consolidated cases or cases in which multiple petitions or amicus briefs have been filed. In such situations, place additional identifying information before the abbreviated name of the court filing. For example:

77-1401 Pet. 23-29. [docket number]

Smith Pet. 14. [petitioner's name]

Jones J.S. App. 15a. [appellant's or appellee's name]

ACLU Amicus Br. [name of amicus]

When introducing page references in citations to court documents *related to the instant case*—at any level—do not use "at" (*e.g.*, "Pet. 5"; "Br. in Opp. 14"; "J.S. 12"; "Gov't C.A. Br. 3"; or "Mem. of P. & A. 9").

Occasionally, however, authors will cite court filings that are not part of the instant case. These citations differ from the citations to court filings in the instant case in several ways: (a) "at" will be included after the abbreviated court filing title and before the page number; (b) a case citation will be included after the cited source; and (c) the docket number will be included if the opinion has been reported. For example:

> Gov't Br. at 9, *Polsby* v. *Shalala*, 113 S. Ct. 1940 (1993) (No. 92-966).

> U.S. Br. at 9, *United States* v. *MacDonald*, No. 80-1582 (Mar. 31, 1982).

> As discussed in our brief (at 9), *Polsby* v. *Shalala*, 113 S. Ct. 1940 (1993) (No. 92-966).

For subsequent citations to court documents not related to the instant case, "*supra*" can be used in place of the case citation:

> Gov't Br. at 10, *Polsby*, *supra* (No. 92-966).

No footnoted explanations are necessary for any of these conventions.

B7.3.1 Court

Do not use the form "Court of Appeals for the Second Circuit." Either use a court's complete formal name, with appropriate capitalization (*e.g.*, "the United States Court of Appeals for the Second Circuit") or use one of the following informal references: (a) "the court of appeals" in lower-case letters, relying on the context to identify the court, or (b) "the District of Columbia Circuit" (or "the D.C. Circuit") or "the Ninth Circuit."

In accordance with longstanding practice, however, we will permit capitalized references to the "Court of Federal Claims," the "Court of Claims" (pre-1982) and the "Claims Court" (1982 onward) rather than "the court of claims" and "the claims court." Authors should endeavor to give the full name of the court ("the United States Claims Court") the first time they refer to this court in each filing.

References to the "Tax Court" are always capitalized.

Court is used instead of Supreme Court.

The name of court, *i.e.*, district court, court of appeals, should be used the first time it is mentioned in the paragraph. In addition, the name of court, *i.e.*, district court, court of appeals, should be provided after court names have been switched for clarity, unless it is clear from the text (for example, "court below").

B7.3.2 Party Designations

Party designations, such as "petitioner," "respondent," "plaintiff," "defendant," "appellant," "appellee," and so forth are not capitalized, even when they refer to the parties in the matter that is the subject of the court document or memorandum.

Do not use a definite article with a party designation that refers to a party in the case in which the document is being filed (*e.g.*, "petitioner," not "the petitioner").

B7.3.3 Titles of Court Documents

Titles of Supreme Court documents appearing in text are not capitalized. The titles are, however, abbreviated when used in citation sentences. This rule applies regardless of whether the reference to the court document is to its official or its generic title. For example, references in text to "petition for a writ of certiorari," or "brief in opposition," are not capitalized. For court documents in all other courts, references are capitalized both in text and in citations. For example:

> The petitioner, in his **Memorandum of Points and Authorities in Opposition to Appellant's Motion to Dismiss,** argued that the Double Jeopardy Clause is not applicable. This argument was renewed in his petition for a writ of certiorari. Pet. 8.

Furthermore, we will continue to use "App." with a capital "A" in referring to appendices.

General Rules of Citation and Style

1 Structure and Use of Citations

1.2 Introductory Signals

Regardless of the context in which they are used, introductory signals are, with one exception, not italicized. That one exception is "*e.g.*," which is italicized when used either by itself or in combination with other signals.

OSG style does not follow the Bluebook rule on grouping/separating families of signals with periods.

Compare v. Cf.:

"Compare" is *only* used with the conjunction "with" when comparing more than one citation. "Compare" is used when comparison of the authorities cited will offer support for or illustrate the proposition.

"Cf." is used when cited authority supports a proposition different from the main proposition but sufficiently analogous to lend support. "Cf." means compare.

For example:

Compare 18 U.S.C. 1963(a), with 18 U.S.C. 1029, 1957.

Compare *Michael H.* v. *Gerald D.*, 491 U.S. 110, 121 (1989) and Catharine A. MacKinnon, *Feminism Unmodified* 49 (1987), with *Loving* v. *Virginia*, 388 U.S. 1, 12 (1967), *Doe* v. *McConn*, 489 F. Supp. 76, 80 (D.D. Tex. 1980), and Kenneth L. Karst, *the Freedom of Intimate Association*, 89 Yale L.J. 624, 638 (1980).

Cf. *United States* v. *Montalvo-Murillo*, 495 U.S. 711 (1990).

1.4 Order of Authorities Within Each Signal

Bluebook Rule 1.4(b) states to put statutes in U.S.C. by progressive order of the U.S.C. title. However, it is common practice for attorneys to list citations with explanatory parentheticals in the order in which they are trying to make a point.

In addition, the following is common practice:

> in violation of 18 U.S.C. 1951(a) and 2

Bluebook Rule 1.4(d) states that for federal court of appeals cases, the order is reverse chronological order. We will follow this rule in addition to arranging federal courts of appeals cases *by circuit order* (1st Cir., 2d Cir., 3d Cir., 4th Cir., 5th Cir., 6th Cir., 7th Cir., 8th Cir., 9th Cir., 10th Cir., 11th Cir., D.C. Cir., Fed. Cir.).

1.5 Parenthetical Information

The following portion of Rule 1.5 is reprinted to emphasize rules which often are not followed:

> Explanatory parenthetical phrases * * * begin with a present participle and should not begin with a capital letter[.] * * * If, however, the parenthetical information quotes one or more full sentences or a portion of material that reads as a full sentence, it should begin with a capital letter and include appropriate closing punctuation[.] * * * [E]xplanatory parenthetical [phrases should] precede any citation of subsequent history or other related authority.

For example:

> Under equivalency analysis, as under literal infringement, the claimed matter must remain the touchstone for a determination of infringement. See *Corning Glass Works*, 868 F.2d at 1259 (**"In the All Elements rule, 'element' is used in the sense of a limitation of a claim."**).

> Under equivalency analysis, as under literal infringement, the claimed matter must remain the touchstone for a determination of infringement. See *Corning Glass*

Works, 868 F.2d at 1259 (**holding that "[i]n the All Elements rule, 'element' is used in the sense of a limitation of a claim"**).

Ibid. (**quoting *American Ass'n of Exporters & Importers* v. *United States*, 583 F. Supp. 591, 598 (Ct. Int'l Trade 1984), aff'd, 751 F.2d 1239, 1247 (Fed. Cir. 1985)**).

Explanatory parentheticals quoting a source will precede explanatory parentheticals containing information about *additions or omissions*. For example:

The court focused on language that gives a national bank authority "to act as a trustee or in a fiduciary capacity 'when not in contravention of [the] State [law] . . . in which the national bank is located.' " Pet. App. 10a (quoting 12 U.S.C. 92a(a)) (brackets in original).

In *Jean*, for example, this Court quoted with approval the Second Circuit's observation that "denying attorneys' fees for time spent in obtaining them would dilute the value of a fees award by forcing attorneys into extensive, uncompensated litigation." 496 U.S. at 162 (quoting *Gagne*, 594 F.2d at 344) (internal quotation marks omitted).

It is a fundamental principle of statutory interpretation that "a word is known by the company it *keeps*." *McDonnell* v. *United States*, 136 S. Ct. 2355, 2368 (2016) (quoting *Jarecki* v. *G. D. Searle & Co.*, 367 U.S. 303, 307 (1961)) (emphasis added).

Explanatory parentheticals containing information about *a quotation with more than one alteration* should include only basic information, omit any duplicative words, and combine words with the conjunction "and" wherever possible. For example:

(citation and footnotes omitted; brackets in original)

NOT:

(citation omitted; footnotes omitted; brackets in original)

BUT (additions will come before omissions):

(citation omitted; emphasis added)

In addition, arrange these in alphabetical order.

(alteration, brackets, citation, emphasis, footnote, and internal quotation marks omitted)

For an internal citation that is omitted, only use "citation omitted." For example:

(citation omitted)

NOT:

(internal citation omitted)

However, when using parenthetical explanatory phrases (or introducing case histories) the repetition of similar phrases is sometimes necessary. For example:

(Powell, J., concurring in part and dissenting in part)

(summary judgment granted in part and denied in part)

(aff'd in part and rev'd in part) [introducing subsequent history]

Explanatory parenthetical phrases immediately follow a citation. But, when the source of a quotation is *part of a textual sentence*, explanatory phrases or citations are placed in parentheses at the end of the sentence to avoid intrusion into the flow of the text. For example:

The Court has jurisdiction of an appeal of "an interlocutory *or* final * * * order * * * holding an Act of Congress unconstitutional" (**28 U.S.C. 1252 (emphasis added)**).

OR:

>Section 1252 gives the Court jurisdiction of an appeal of "an interlocutory *or* final * * * order * * * holding an Act of Congress unconstitutional." **28 U.S.C. 1252 (emphasis added)**.

NOT:

>Section 1252 **(emphasis added)** gives the Court jurisdiction of an appeal of "an interlocutory *or* final * * * order * * * holding an Act of Congress unconstitutional."

When an explanatory parenthetical contains a quote, nesting is also not followed. For example:

>See 28 U.S.C. 1254(1) (providing that courts of appeals' decisions may be reviewed "[b]y writ of certiorari granted upon the petition of *any* party to *any* civil or criminal case") (emphases added).

NOT:

>See 28 U.S.C. 1254(1) (providing that courts of appeals' decisions may be reviewed "[b]y writ of certiorari granted upon the petition of any party to any civil or criminal case" (emphases added)).

When an explanatory parenthetical contains a quote that was quoted from a source, (quoting source) or (citation omitted) will follow the explanatory parenthetical and will not be nested. For example:

>The court then reviewed each statement that petitioner challenged. Pet. App. 12a (agent's comments that petitioner was "a tough guy") (citation omitted).

NOT:

>The court then reviewed each statement that petitioner challenged. Pet. App. 12a (citation omitted) (agent's comments that petitioner was "a tough guy").

NOT:

> The court then reviewed each statement that petitioner challenged.   Pet. App. 12a (agent's comments that petitioner was "a tough guy" (citation omitted)).

The same principles should be followed when the source precedes an indented quotation.   Examples:

> The statute provides (§ 105(a), 60 Stat. 433 (emphasis added)):
>
> > The maximum lawful price *computed under subsection (b)* * * * .

OR:

> Section 105(a), in pertinent part, states:
>
> > The maximum lawful price *computed under subsection (b)* * * * .
>
> § 105(a), 60 Stat. 433 (emphasis added).

1.6   Related Authority

1.6(a)(ii) *"Reprinted In"*

Because it is OSG's practice to cite only original sources and not additionally to a reprinting, citations typically will not include the phrase *"reprinted in."*   For example, no citation is made to U.S.C.C.A.N. for congressional materials that are reprinted therein.

However, citations to separately bound legislative histories may be retained when useful (*e.g.*, S. Rep. No. 813, 89th Cong., 1st Sess. 3 (1965), *reprinted in* Staff of the Subcomm. on Administrative Practice and Procedure, Senate Comm. on the Judiciary, 93d Cong., 2d Sess., *Freedom of Information Act Source Book: Legislative Materials, Cases, Articles* 38 (Comm. Print 1974)).

Note: OSG style uses both "Congress" and "Session" and therefore deviates from Bluebook Rule 13, which does not include the "Session."

2 Typefaces for Law Reviews

Only two typefaces are used. Titles are in italics (or underlined). The rest of the citation is Roman (with Arabic numerals):

> Timothy M. Cook, *The Americans with Disabilities Act: The Move to Integration*, 64 Temp. L. Rev. 393 (1991).

> Louis Loss, *The SEC Proxy Rules in the Courts*, 73 Harv. L. Rev. 1041 (1960).

3 Subdivisions

3.1 Volumes, Parts, and Supplements

3.1(c) Supplements

When citing the United States Code, include a date only for clarity or if the cited section derives from a supplement, from a volume *not* part of the most recent full edition of the Code, or from an edition other than the most recent full edition of the Code. The supplement used is the most current supplement, unless a specific year is needed. For example:

> 18 U.S.C. 2. [example that is found only in main volume of the most recent Code]

> 52 U.S.C. 10101 (Sup. III 2015). [example that is found only in a supplement]

> 29 U.S.C. 794 (2012 & Supp. IV 2016). [example that is found in both the main volume and a supplement]

When an entire act is cited by the use of "*et seq.*," do not include a date even if portions of the act are contained in more recent supplements. For example:

> Immigration and Nationality Act, 8 U.S.C. 1101 *et seq.*

NOT:

> Immigration and Nationality Act, 8 U.S.C. 1101 *et seq.* (2012 & Supp. IV 2016).

BUT:

> Voting Rights Act of 1965, 52 U.S.C. 1101 *et seq.* (Supp. III 2015).

When citing material in federal and state statutes, cite pocket parts and bound supplements as "Supp." (retain all other normal identifying words).   For example:

> Mo. Ann. Stat. § 514.140 (West Supp. 1984).

NOT:

> Mo. Ann. Stat. § 514.140 (West Cum. Pocket Pt. 1984).

3.2   Pages, Footnotes, Endnotes, and Graphical Materials

3.2(a) Pages

When citing court filings *in the instant case*, place the cited page numbers directly after the abbreviated name of the court filing, without using the word "at" (*e.g.*, Pet. App. 3a; Pet. 19; C.A. E.R. 46-50; U.S. Br. 9; J.S. 20; J.A. 300-345; Mot. to Affirm 9; GX 3; or 6/19/84 Tr. 9).   However, use ", at" to distinguish a page number from a *numbered document* (*e.g.*, Doc. 12, at 20; or C.R. 12, at 20 (this is an example of a numbered document in the Ninth Circuit original record; original paging is retained)).   When using this form, always include the comma prior to "at."

When there is a miscellaneous source, such as Senate Report or a book, that has been given a short form, do not use "at page number."   For example:

> Senate Report 5.

> *Collier* 2.

Also, use "at" in parenthetical citations set off from the text when the surrounding context has already identified the court document. For example:

As we stated earlier in our petition (at 3) * * * .

BUT:

As we stated earlier (Pet. 3) * * * .

Furthermore, use "at" when citing pages using "*id.*" (*e.g.*, *id.* at 9a.). Do not, however, use "at" with "*id.*" when citing sections (§), paragraphs (¶), etc.

Citations of a *section* or *act* contained in the Statutes at Large should identify the page on which the section or act begins. Citations of a *portion* of a section should include only the page(s) on which the relevant material appears.

Citations of the *Federal Register* should include *BOTH* the first page on which a document begins and the relevant page. For example:

65 Fed. Reg. 70,246 70,250 (Nov. 21, 2000).

Note that the TOA will only have the citation including the first page on which a document begins, and not the individual pages listed. The individual pages will be paginated the same ay as any other miscellaneous source is paginated. For example, the citation in the TOA would be, for the above example:

65 Fed. Reg. 70,246 (Nov. 21, 2000)

When a brief contains multiple appendices, do not cite a specific appendix (*e.g.*, J.S. App. A, Pet. App. D) except in unusual circumstances (*e.g.*, when multiple appendices are separately paginated, citations to a specific appendix are necessary). As long as the appendix pages are consecutively or distinctively numbered, it is accurate and helpful to the reader to identify the range of specific page numbers when referring to the particular appendix. Thus:

The court of appeals affirmed.   Pet. App. 1a-45a.

NOT:

The court of appeals affirmed.   Pet. App. A.

When citing pages from another party's appendix, eliminate unnecessary hyphens.   Thus, even if an appendix is paginated "1-a" or "A-1," refer to "1a" or "A1."   This will avoid awkward forms (*e.g.*, Pet. App. 1-a to 4-a.).   It is also acceptable to collapse appendix names and numbering (*e.g.*, Pet. App. B4 rather than Pet. App. B, at 4).

For citation of pages as internal cross-references, see Rule 3.5.

Contrary to Rule 3.3(b) repetitious digits will not be dropped when citing multiple pages and/or footnotes.   For example:

88 Harv. L. Rev. 1127, 1130-1136 & nn.106-107.

NOT:

88 Harv. L. Rev. 1127, 1130-36 & nn.106-07.

"*Et seq.*" is not used when referring to multiple pages.   Rather, "*et seq.*" is used only when referring to multiple sections or paragraphs.   For example:

National Environmental Policy Act of 1969, Pub. L. No. 91-190, 83 Stat. 852.

NOT:

National Environmental Policy Act of 1969, Pub. L. No. 91-190, 83 Stat. 852 *et seq.*

3.2(b) Footnotes

The OSG style for citing footnotes that span more than one page is the same as that in the Bluebook, but confusion exists concerning its application.   Rule 3.2(b) reads (emphases added):

To cite [*all* of] a footnote that spans more than one page, cite only the page on which the footnote *begins*, "n.," and the footnote number[.] * * * When referring only to *specific pages* of a footnote that spans more than one page, cite only the specific pages, rather than the page on which the footnote begins[.]

When citing a range of pages, as well as a footnote on a page within that range, two choices exist. Either cite the page range followed by an ampersand (&), "n.," and the footnote number, or cite the page range, followed by the page on which the footnote begins, "n.," and the footnote number. For example:

Pet. Br. 3-5 & n.1.

OR

Pet. Br. 3-5, 4 n.1.

When a filing has only one footnote in the text, an asterisk (*) is used in lieu of a footnote number. Also, asterisks are used in lieu of footnote numbers in the "Question Presented," "Parties to the Proceeding," and signature-block sections. The numeral one (1) will then be used for a single footnote in the text.

3.3 Sections and Paragraphs

Section symbols (§) are not used in citations to the U.S.C. or C.F.R. We will use the section symbol in citations to federal and state session laws and state codes that use section symbols. For example:

42 U.S.C. 2000e.

7 C.F.R. 1962.5.

Buck Act, ch. 787, § 7, 54 Stat. 1060.

Airline Deregulation Act of 1978, Pub. L. No. 95-504, § 20(d)(1), 92 Stat. 1722.

Act of Apr. 25, 1978, No. 515, § 3, 1978 Ala. Acts 569.

Iowa Code § 235A.1 (1994).

Rule 12.4(d) regarding session laws amending prior acts will now be followed. This rule provides that (emphases added):

> Session laws amending prior acts are often divided into sections within sections; that is, the session law is divided into primary sections, and these sections, in turn, contain sections of the amended act. Cite the *bill's* sections by abbreviation (sec.) and the *amended act's* sections by symbol (§):

> Labor-Management Relations Act, ch. 120, sec. 101, § 8(a)(3), 61 Stat. 140-141.

As a general rule, section symbols are not used in text; rather, spell out the word "Section." An exception to this rule is when a quote uses a section symbol in the quoted text. An additional exception to this rule and Rule 12.9.5 occurs referring to specific sentencing guidelines in accordance with the following examples:

> **Sentencing Guidelines § 1B1.3** provides that * * * .

> The en banc court of appeals held that **Sentencing Guidelines § 1B1.3** requires * * * .

BUT:

> **Section 1B1.3** provides * * * .

> The en banc court of appeals stated that Section 1B1.3 should be interpreted as * * * .

When citing an individual paragraph in a source, the written abbreviation ("para.") should be used when the source itself does not number its paragraphs. When the source uses numbered paragraphs, they may be cited with a paragraph symbol (¶) even if that symbol does not appear next to the numbers in the source (as is commonly the case with Presentence Investigation Reports, pleadings, declarations, affidavits, and orders by administrative agencies).

3.3(b) **Multiple Sections and Subsections**

We will use "*et seq.*" in citing multiple sections of statutes or regulations when a precise range of section numbers is not needed for clarity (*e.g.*, Administrative Procedure Act, 5 U.S.C. 551 *et seq.*).   In compilations that use section symbols (§), the symbol should be used twice for "*et seq.*" citations: "D.C. Code Ann. §§ 36-301 *et seq.*"

We will not drop digits in citing multiple sections or paragraphs (8 U.S.C. 2113, 2114, 2115).   We will, however, continue to drop repetitive digits and letters when citing a number of *subsections*, unless this produces a confusing citation. In addition, we will substitute the word "and" for what would be the comma separating the last two cited *subsections*.

For example:

> 18 U.S.C. 2113(a) and (d).

> 18 U.S.C. 2113(a), (b), and (d).

> 18 U.S.C. 2113(a)-(d).

> 18 U.S.C. 2113 (a)(1) and (d).

> 18 U.S.C. 1936a-1936d.   [NOT: 18 U.S.C. 1936a-d, which would be confusing]

> 7 C.F.R. 1980.170(a), (b)(1), and (3).

Multiple paragraphs should be treated like multiple sections.

> 1 Blue Sky L. Rep. (CCH) ¶¶ 4471-4474.

3.4 **Appended Material**

Notwithstanding Rule 3.4, we will continue to use "App." with a capital "A" in referring to statutory and other appendices.

When citing pages from another party's appendix, eliminate unnecessary hyphens. For example, even if an appendix is paginated "1-a" or "A-1," refer to "1a" or "A1." This will avoid awkward forms (*e.g.*, Pet. App. 1-a to 4-a.). It is also acceptable to collapse appendix names and numbering (*e.g.*, Pet. App. B4 rather than Pet. App. B, at 4).

For additional rules on how to cite to appendices, see Rules 3.2(a) and 10.8.3.

3.5   Internal Cross-References

Despite Rule 3.5, we will continue to cross-reference portions of text and footnotes by placing "*supra*" or "*infra*" *after* the page or note being cross-referenced:

> See p. 41, *supra.*

> See p. 18 n.4, *infra.*

> See also pp. 43-44, *supra.*

> See Part I, *infra.*

> See Part I.B.1, *infra.*

"Page" and "footnote" will generally be abbreviated "p." and "n.," but "part" will be spelled out.

Use the form "App., *infra*, 1a-5a" or "App., *infra*" when citing an appendix *bound together* with the brief it accompanies. For citations to *separately bound* appendices, use the following form without "*infra*" (descriptive names, numbers, etc. can be added):

> App. 18a.

> Pet. App 32a.

> 02-1222 Pet. App. 133.

> Resp. Exxon App. 12a.

4 Short Citation Forms

Short citation forms (*e.g.*, *id.* at) will usually include "at" preceding the specific page number. However, if what is being referenced is not a page but a section (§) or paragraph (¶), "at" is not used. For example:

Church of Scientology, 506 U.S. at 10.

506 U.S. at 11.

Id. at 9.

Church of Scientology, slip op. 3.

Gov't Br. 26.

Id. at 27.

Tribe § 26. [a book]

Id. § 27.

Collier 45. [a book]

135 Cong. Rec. at 23,420.

4.1 "*Id.*"

The use of "*id.* at" and "*ibid.*" should be limited to instances where the immediately preceding citation refers to the same authority. In other words, if there is an intervening citation to a different authority, then a subsequent citation to a previously cited authority should be cited in full or in an appropriate short form. *Note*: explanatory parentheticals do not count as intervening citations.

"*Id.*" and "*ibid.*" cannot be carried into subsequent paragraphs. A full citation must be recited in each new paragraph.

For purposes of this rule, it should be understood that a mere textual reference to a constitutional, statutory, or regulatory provision, case name, etc., need *not* be regarded as an intervening citation. For example:

> The court of appeals affirmed. **Pet. App. 1a-18a. Relying on *Smith*,** the court upheld the application of Section 201 to this case, ***id.* at 4a,** and rejected petitioner's challenge under the Due Process Clause, ***ibid.***

NOT:

> The court of appeals affirmed. **Pet. App. 1a-18a. Relying on *Smith*,** the court upheld the application of Section 201 to this case, **Pet. App. 4a,** and rejected petitioner's challenge under the Due Process Clause, **Pet. App. 4a.**

Sources identified in explanatory parentheticals are ignored for purposes of determining whether to use "*id.* at" or "*ibid.*" For example:

> The court recognized that deference is not owed to an agency's interpretation of a statutory scheme it is charged with administering. **Pet. App. 12a (citing *Chevron*, 467 U.S. at 843-844).** The court concluded that the agency's construction of Section 201 was a reasonable one. ***Id.* at 14a.**

NOT:

> The court recognized that deference is not owed to an agency's interpretation of a statutory scheme it is charged with administering. **Pet. App. 12a (citing *Chevron*, 467 U.S. at 843-844).** The court concluded that the agency's construction of Section 201 was a reasonable one. **Pet. App. 14a.**

We will depart from Bluebook Rule 4.1 to the extent that we will use "*ibid.*" when citing to the same authority and same page (or section, or paragraph) as in the immediately preceding citation. *Ibid.* is used with "Tr.," "Pet.," "PSR," "A.R.," "GX," "J.A.," or "Br." in consecutive citations. However, "*id.* at" is not used with "Tr.," "Pet.," PSR," "A.R.," "GX,"

"J.A.," or "Br." in consecutive citations. But "*id.* at" is used with "Pet. Br." or "Resp. Br." in consecutive citations.

For example:

> Petitioner contends (Br. 12-22) that * * * . Petitioner also argues (Br. 28-30) that * * * .

NOT:

> Petitioner contends (Br. 12-22) that * * * . Petitioner also argues (*id.* at 28-30) that * * * .

For example:

> Petitioner contends (Br. 12-22) that * * * . Petitioner's reliance on Fourth Circuit precedent is also misplaced. Pet. Br. 23-27 (citing cases).

NOT:

> Petitioner contends (Br. 12-22) that * * * . Petitioner's reliance on Fourth Circuit precedent is also misplaced. *Id.* at 23-27 (citing cases).

For example:

> Petitioner states that * * * . Pet. Br. 22 (quoting 18 U.S.C. 924). Petitioner's reliance on Fourth Circuit precedent is also misplaced. *Id.* at 23-27 (citing cases).

NOT:

> Petitioner states that * * * . Pet. Br. 22 (quoting 18 U.S.C. 924). Petitioner's reliance on Fourth Circuit precedent is also misplaced. Pet. Br. 23-27 (citing cases).

Neither "*id.* at" nor "*ibid.*" is used to refer to a source that is part of a citation sentence containing more than one citation. "*Ibid.*" can be used to refer to *all* of the sources identified in a previous citation sentence containing multiple sources, provided that the latter citation also refers to *all of the same pages in the prior citations.*

For example:

> Petitioner argued in the court of appeals and the district court that * * * . **Pet. App. 3a; C.A. App. 340.** Petitioner further argued that * * * . ***Ibid.*** [*Note: Ibid.* refers to both Pet. App. 3a and C.A. App. 340.]

For example:

> Petitioner argued in the court of appeals and the district court that * * * . **Pet. App. 3a; C.A. App. 340.** Petitioner further argued that * * * . **C.A. App. 340.**

> Petitioner argued in the court of appeals and the district court that * * * . **Pet. App. 3a; C.A. App. 340.** Petitioner further argued that * * * . ***Id.* at 340.**

The Bluebook allows for the use of "*id.* § X" when citing a different section of the same work cited in the immediately preceding citation. This format ("*id.*" without the word "at") may also be used when citing other organized segments (*e.g.*, ch., §, ¶, para., Pt., Subpt., Tbl., Ex., etc.) of a work. This rule, however, shall not be applied to statutory or regulatory sections in the United States Code or C.F.R. For those sources, "*id.* at" is not an appropriate short form (although "*ibid.*" is).

4.2 "*Supra*" and "Hereinafter"

4.2(a) "*Supra*"

Generally, "*supra*" is *not* used. There are two narrow exceptions to this rule: internal cross-references and cases cited generally.

In most instances, "*supra*" shall not be used to refer to cases previously cited. However, we will use "*supra*" when we use the case name without a page citation. A case may be cited in its entirety with its full name and "*supra*" (*e.g.*, *Wuchter* v.

Pizzutti, supra), but if the case name is long, it is not necessary to repeat it entirely. A previously introduced short citation may be used with *supra* as well. For example, *Valley Forge, supra*, would be an acceptable substitute for *Valley Forge Christian College* v. *Americans United for Separation of Church and State, Inc., supra*.

Inclusion of "*supra*" may also be appropriate if the attorney wishes to ensure that the citation will be noted in the table of authorities (which otherwise does not include page references to cases that are mentioned only textually).

For internal cross-references, see Rule 3.5.

4.2(b) "Hereinafter"

We depart from the Bluebook in that the word "hereinafter" is *not* used to introduce a short form for an authority that would be cumbersome to cite repeatedly. Instead, a short name will be introduced in parentheses (*without* quotation marks) immediately following the source, and the shortened form shall be in the same typeface as the source. For example:

> *Proposed Amendments to the Federal Rules of Criminal Procedure: Hearings Before the Subcomm. on Criminal Justice of the House Comm. on the Judiciary*, 95th Cong., 1st Sess. 93 (1977) (***Hearings***).

Subsequent references use the defined short form with the appropriate page, section, or paragraph (without the word "at" or "*supra*"):

> *Hearings* 95.

5 Quotations

5.1 Formatting of Quotations

When quoting language that is itself *entirely* a quotation, do not enclose the quotation in both double (") and single (') quotation marks; double quotation marks alone will do. For example:

In *Mead*, the Court stated that "[i]f the intent of Congress is clear, that is the end of the matter." *Mead Corp.* v. *Tilley*, 490 U.S. at 722 (quoting *Chevron U.S.A. Inc.* v. *NRDC, Inc.*, 467 U.S. 837, 842-843 (1987)).

NOT:

In *Mead*, the Court stated that "'[i]f the intent of Congress is clear, that is the end of the matter.'" *Mead Corp.* v. *Tilley*, 490 U.S. at 722 (quoting *Chevron U.S.A. Inc.* v. *NRDC, Inc.*, 467 U.S. 837, 842-843 (1987)).

In the first example, it is not necessary to indicate parenthetically "internal quotation marks omitted." See Rule 5.3. The office preference is to indicate parenthetically the original sources of "quotes within quotes," but (citation omitted) is also allowed.

When needed to distinguish quoted material from a quotation of a *quotation*, however, single and double quotation marks *must* be used.

In *Mead*, the Court addressed whether ERISA "requires a plan administrator to pay plan participants unreduced early retirement benefits provided under the plan before residual assets may revert to an employer," stating that "'[i]f the intent of Congress is clear, that is the end of the matter.'" *Mead Corp.* v. *Tilley*, 490 U.S. at 722 (quoting *Chevron U.S.A. Inc.* v. *NRDC, Inc.*, 467 U.S. 837, 842-843 (1987)).

NOT:

In *Mead*, the Court addressed whether ERISA "requires a plan administrator to pay plan participants unreduced early retirement benefits provided under the plan before residual assets may revert to an employer," stating that "[i]f the intent of Congress is clear, that is the end of the matter." *Mead Corp.* v. *Tilley*, 490 U.S. at 722 (quoting *Chevron U.S.A. Inc.* v. *NRDC, Inc.*, 467 U.S. 837, 842-843 (1987)).

We will use double quotation marks ("), not single quotation marks ('), for material quoted within *indented* quotations (which do not begin or end with quotation marks). No explanatory parenthetical is needed, nor are any brackets needed to indicate this alteration.

Citations may either precede or follow indented quotations. Citations following an indented quotation are to be aligned with the left margin in the line immediately following the quotation.

5.1(a),
5.1(b) **Quotations of More Than 50 Words; Quotations 50 or Fewer Words**

This office deviates slightly from the Bluebook rule, in that we will follow Supreme Court Rule 33.1(b), which requires quotations *in excess of* 50 words to be indented. Whether to indent shorter quotations remains a matter of judgment for the author. When indenting quotations that are in excess of 50 words, only indent the block quote on the left side.

5.2 **Alterations and Quotations Within Quotations**

Alterations to a quotation must be indicated by the use of brackets.

We will use double quotation marks ("), not single quotation marks ('), for material quoted within *indented* quotations, which do not begin or end with quotation marks.

Alteration of the emphasis in the original text is indicated in a parenthetical following the quote with either "emphasis added" or "emphasis omitted." If the emphasis of the original text is not altered, do *not* indicate in a parenthetical "emphasis in original." A quotation is presumed to be unaltered unless an alteration is noted.

Any parenthetical that indicates alteration of a quotation contained in a parenthetical should directly follow the quotation and precede any subsequent history. For example:

Campbell v. *Fair*, 838 F.2d 1, 4 (1st Cir.) ("*Mere* presence at the scene of the crime, of course, is not evidence of guilt.") **(emphasis added)**, cert. denied, No. 88-3 (Oct. 3, 1988).

NOT:

Campbell v. *Fair*, 838 F.2d 1, 4 (1st Cir.) ("*Mere* presence at the scene of the crime, of course, is not evidence of guilt."), cert. denied, No. 88-3 (Oct. 3, 1988) **(emphasis added)**.

Changes in tense or changes to a single word, such as a change from "defendant" to "[petitioner]," are not omissions but substitutions, and need not be indicated with the use of asterisks (* * *).   Instead, the substituted word is placed in brackets.

For omissions of citations, footnotes, and internal quotation marks, see Rule 5.3.   For structure of the parentheticals, see Rule 1.5.

5.3   Omissions

Notwithstanding Bluebook Rule 5.3, we will insert two spaces before the first and after the last period (...) and insert one hard space between the ellipsis.   The same is true for alterations made by OSG with the use of asterisks (* * *).

Despite the Bluebook's endorsement of the ellipsis as a symbol for omissions from quotations, we will continue to use the asterisk form (* * *) that we have used in the past.   The use of the asterisks eliminates any problem in determining whether a quoted sentence ends before or after an omission. However, an ellipsis contained within quoted material should not be translated into asterisks.

An omission *at the end of a quoted sentence* should not be indicated by asterisks between the last word quoted and the final punctuation of the sentence quoted.

If language *after the end of a quoted sentence* is deleted and the sentence is followed by further quotation, retain the punctuation at the end of the sentence and insert asterisks before the remainder of the quotation:

> "The need to develop all relevant facts in the adversary system is both fundamental and comprehensive. * * * [I]t is imperative to the function of the courts that compulsory process be available for the production of evidence needed either by the prosecution or by the defense."

If language *both at the end and after the end* of a quoted sentence is deleted and followed by further quotation, place the final punctuation mark of the quoted sentence in brackets and use only *one* set of asterisks to indicate both of the omissions:

> "The need to develop all relevant facts in the adversary system is * * * **fundamental[.]** * * * [I]t is imperative to the function of the courts that compulsory process be available for the production of evidence needed either by the prosecution or by the defense."

Per Bluebook Rule 5.3, certain omissions need not be indicated by asterisks. For example, omitted citations, footnotes, or internal quotation marks need not be indicated by asterisks; a parenthetical stating "internal citation omitted," "footnote omitted," or "internal quotation marks omitted" suffices. Thus:

> "[W]hether the government floods a landowner's property, *Pumpelly* v. *Green Bay Co.*, 13 Wall. 166 (1872), or does no more than require the landowner to suffer the installation of a cable, *Loretto*, *supra*, the Takings Clause requires compensation if the government authorizes a compelled physical invasion of property." *Yee* v. *Escondido*, 503 U.S. 519, 527 (1992).

can properly be quoted as:

"[W]hether the government floods a landowner's property, or does no more than require the landowner to suffer the installation of a cable, the Takings Clause requires compensation if the government authorizes a compelled physical invasion of property." *Yee* v. *Escondido*, 503 U.S. 519, 527 (1992) **(internal citations omitted)**.

We will not use "footnote omitted" to indicate that a footnote number that follows the last word quoted has been omitted. We will also not use "footnote omitted" if the footnote consists of only a citation; instead "citation omitted" will be used.

We will follow the Bluebook by attributing a quotation within a quotation to the original source. However, if this is not possible, or the attorney does not want to do this, we will use "citation omitted" to indicate that we have not attributed a quotation within a quotation to its original source. We will also use "citation omitted" when we have omitted a citation from quoted material without so indicating by asterisks. Thus, either of the following forms suffices:

> Justice White's dissent in *Tarkanian* indicated that "the NCAA was 'jointly engaged with [UNLV] officials in the challenged action,' and therefore was a state actor." Slip op. 3 **(citation omitted)**.

> Justice White's dissent in *Tarkanian* indicated that "the NCAA was 'jointly engaged with [UNLV] officials in the challenged action,' and therefore was a state actor." Slip op. 3 (quoting *Dennis* v. *Sparks*, 449 U.S. 24, 27-28 (1980)). **[This is the preferred style.]**

For structure of parentheticals, see Rule 1.5.

6   Abbreviations, Numerals, and Symbols

6.1   Abbreviations

Generally, follow the Bluebook's abbreviations, as set forth in the Tables (*19th edition of the Bluebook*). In text, however, abbreviations are disfavored.

Paralegals should spell out case names in text and abbreviate them in citations. However, it is ultimately the author's decision whether or not to abbreviate words in case names. When a word in a case name is abbreviated, the abbreviations listed in Bluebook T6, at 430-431 govern.

There are four exceptions to this rule as applied to case names:

First, do not abbreviate the first word of a party's name.

> *Coleman* v. *American Red Cross*, 23 F. 3d 1091 (6th Cir. 1994).

NOT:

> *Coleman* v. *Am. Red Cross*, 23 F. 3d 1091 (6th Cir. 1994).

Second, abbreviate words to achieve consistency throughout a brief. Once a word in a case name has been abbreviated, that same word is to be abbreviated wherever it appears in any case citation (except when it is the first word in a party's name).

Third, several words *always* appear as abbreviations in case names: &, Ass'n, Bros., Co., Corp., Inc., Int'l, Ltd., and No. For additional rules pertaining to abbreviation of case names, see Rule 10.2.

Fourth, when case names are used textually (in sentences), abbreviations will not be used, except for: &, Ass'n, Bros., Co., Corp., Inc., Int'l, Ltd., and No.

Bluebook BT1, at 28-29 (*19th edition of the Bluebook*) sets forth the abbreviations to be followed in court documents.

For business firm designations, follow the *19th edition of the Bluebook*: omit Inc., Ltd., L.L.C., N.A., F.S.B., and similar terms if the name also contains a word such as Ass'n, Bros., Co., Corp., or R.R., clearly indicating that the party is a business firm. See Rule 10.2.1(h).

For example:

> *Wisconsin Packing Co.* v. *Indiana Refrigerator Lines, Inc.*

NOT:

> *Wisconsin Packing Co., Inc.* v. *Indiana Refrigerator Lines, Inc.*

For example:

> *Winans* v. *New York & Erie R.R.*, 62 U.S. (21 How.) 88 (1859).

NOT:

> *Winans* v. *New York & Erie R.R. Co.*, 62 U.S. (21 How.) 88 (1859).

BUT:

> *Great N. Ry. Co.* v. *Merchants Elevator Co.*, 259 U.S. 285 (1922).

6.2   Numerals and Symbols

6.2(a),   Numerals; Ordinals
6.2(b)

Despite Rule 6.2, we will spell out the numbers from zero through ten (*not* through 99) and use numerals for larger numbers.   We will follow the exceptions to this rule as noted in 6.2(a).   For example, round numbers will ordinarily be written out when they are used to indicate approximations; numbers that begin a sentence will always be written out; and numerals will be used where one or more of the numbers in a series exceeds ten.   Additionally, numerals will be used in counts of an indictment or complaint (*e.g.*, Count 1).

When referring to dates in text, use numbers, not ordinals. For example, refer to "September 4," not "September 4th."

The same principle applies in citations, except that in citations the month will be abbreviated as prescribed in Bluebook T12, at 444 (*e.g.*, Sept. 4, 1996).

Numbers of five or more digits (including page or paragraph numbers in citations) require commas to separate groups of three digits. Thus, cite "40 Fed. Reg. 56,895," not "40 Fed. Reg. 56895." Exception: U.S. Senate or House bill numbers of five digits or more (*e.g.*, H.R. 11267) do not take commas. Do not use commas in four-digit numbers.

When ordinals are used (*e.g.*, when indicating which circuit decided a case in a citation), follow the Bluebook and refer to "2d" and "3d," rather than "2nd" and "3rd."

Refer to particular hours of the day as follows:

9 a.m.

NOT:

9:00 am.

6.2(c) **Section (§) and Paragraph (¶) Symbols**

Section symbols (§) are not used in citations to the U.S.C. or C.F.R. However, use the section symbol when citing federal and state session laws and state codes that use section symbols. For example:

42 U.S.C. 2000e.

7 C.F.R. 1962.5.

Buck Act, ch. 787, § 7, 54 Stat. 1060.

Airline Deregulation Act of 1978, Pub. L. No. 95-504, § 20(d)(1), 92 Stat. 1722.

Act of Apr. 25, 1978, No. 515, § 3, 1978 Ala. Acts 569.

Iowa Code § 235A.1 (1994).

Rule 12.4(d) regarding session laws amending prior acts will now be followed. This rule provides that (emphasis added):

> Session laws amending prior acts are often divided into sections within sections; that is, the session law is divided into primary sections, and these sections, in turn, contain sections of the amended act. Cite the *bill's* sections by abbreviation (sec.) and the *amended act's* sections by symbol (§):

> Labor-Management Relations Act, ch. 120, sec. 101, § 8(a)(3), 61 Stat. 140-141.

As a general rule, section symbols are not used in text; rather, spell out the word "section." An exception to this rule occurs when referring to specific sentencing guidelines in accordance with the following examples:

> **Sentencing Guidelines § 1B1.3** provides that * * * .

> The en banc court of appeals held that Sentencing Guidelines § 1B1.3 requires * * * .

BUT:

> Section 1B1.3 provides * * * .

> The en banc court of appeals stated that Section 1B1.3 should be interpreted as * * * .

6.2(d) Dollar ($) and Percent (%) Symbols

When referring to large amounts of money, do not use the pure words or pure numbers forms in Bluebook Rule 6.2(d). Rather, use the form "$65 million." Generally, round off large sums; in any event, refer to even dollars as $5, not $5.00.

7 Italicization for Style and in Unique Circumstances

7(b) Foreign words and phrases

Despite the strong presumption of Bluebook Rule 7(b) against italicizing Latin words and phrases, we will continue to italicize *a fortiori, e.g., et seq., i.e., infra, inter alia, passim, sic., sub nom.,* and *supra.* In addition, because the Court itself usually italicizes Latin phrases, the italicization of such phrases will generally be up to the individual author's preference and should not be altered by paralegals. A few phrases, however, are used so frequently in legal writing and have become so incorporated into English usage that we will not italicize them. These are certiorari, mandamus, habeas, per se, pro se, ad hoc, and status quo. Similarly, we will not italicize the phrase en banc (or its variant in banc), per curiam, or mens rea.

The lowercase letters "l" and "o" will be italicized when used as a subsection. For example:

42 U.S.C. 2000e-2(*l*).

42 U.S.C. 2000e-2(*o*).

But the lowercase letter "i" will not be italicized or underscored when used as a subsection. For example:

42 U.S.C. 200e-2(i).

8　Capitalization

In addition to the notes below, Bluepages B7.3, with its rules on capitalization concerning court documents, party designations, and courts, provides further assistance on capitalization. For other words, use the table of capitalizations in the U.S. Government Printing Office Style Manual (2008), http://www.gpo.gov/fdsys/pkg/GPO-STYLEMANUAL-2008/pdf/GPO-STYLEMANUAL-2008.pdf.

Appendix　　　Refer to appendices, statutory and otherwise, as "App." with a capital "A."

Chapter, Subchapter	The words "Chapter" and "Subchapter," when referring to regulations, legislative materials, or other materials, will be abbreviated "Ch." and "Subchap." and capitalized (*e.g.*, 35 U.S.C. Ch. 2). However, when citing *session laws* from the U.S. Statutes at Large, references to chapter numbers will be abbreviated "ch." and *not* capitalized (*e.g.*, White-Slave Traffic (Mann) Act, ch. 395, 36 Stat. 825). See Bluebook Rule 12.4.
Constitution	Despite Rule 8, references to part of a constitution (federal, state, or foreign) will be capitalized in both text *and citations*. For example, we will refer in the text to the Fifth Amendment and Article III courts. Rule 11 will be followed in citations, except that the parts are to be capitalized (*e.g.*, U.S. Const. Art. I, § 8, Cl. 5).
Government	When referring to the federal government as a party, do not capitalize the word "government."
Judge, Justice	"Judge" or "Justice" is capitalized only when referring to a Justice or Justices of the Supreme Court of the United States, or when referring to any judge by name. For example:

> The case was argued before a panel of three **judges**.   In his opinion, **Judge** Posner wrote * * * .

> The case was argued before eight **Justices**.

In addition, even though "ALJ" is a commonly used abbreviation, refer to the "administrative law judge," without capital letters.

Section, Subsection	The words "Section," "Subsection," and "Rule," when referring to statutes and rules of procedure, evidence, bankruptcy, etc., will be capitalized. So will "Act," whether or not it refers to a specific statute.

Part, Subpart, Title, Subtitle	The words "Part" and "Subpart," when referring to regulations, legislative materials, or other materials will be capitalized. They will be abbreviated in citations as "Pt." and "Subpt." "Title" and "Subtitle," when referring to regulations, legislative materials, or other materials, will be capitalized and will be abbreviated in citations as "Tit." and "Subtit."
State, Nation, Executive	Capitalize "State(s)" and "Nation" whenever they are used as nouns to refer to one or more of the States or the United States, respectively. Do not capitalize "state" or "national" when used as an adjective, unless part of a proper name. Thus, "the State Commissioner," "the National Guard," "the state interest," and "the State argued in the court of appeals" are proper applications of the capitalization rule. Similarly, capitalize "Executive" only when used as a noun, not as an adjective. Likewise, do not capitalize "federal" or "congressional" unless part of a proper name. For example:

> The Senate Report clearly indicated the **congressional** intent * * * .

> The Senator's statements were not floor statements, but extensions of remarks placed in the ***Congressional*** *Record*.

Ship names, Aircraft, etc.	Use italics with an initial capital letter for the names of ships and aircraft but do not place preceding names or abbreviations in italics. For example:

> the *Millennium Falcon*

> USS *Enterprise*

9   Titles of Judges, Officials, and Terms of Court

See Rule 8 regarding capitalization of "judge" or "justice."

For short forms to cases, clarity and ease in locating a full citation are the governing principles.   There are instances in which a full citation is required or preferred.   It is an attorney's discretion whether to use a short form for a case.   A full citation must be used the first time a case is cited in the brief.   If a case is cited for the first time in a footnote, however, the source must be cited in full *both* in the footnote and where it first appears in the text.[2]

Although attorney preference and space constraints may dictate otherwise, it is preferred that a case be cited in full the first time it is cited in the statement of interest, statement, summary of argument, and argument/discussion sections of the brief.   If a short form is used, it is the attorney's discretion as to whether it appears with the full citation for the first time in the statement, summary of argument, or argument/discussion sections.   Subsequent citations in the same section may take that short form.

If a short form is used, the location of the short form would appear after the citation and before any subsequent history. For example:

> *Voest-Alpine Trading USA Corp.* v. *Bank of China*, 142 F.3d 887, 890 (5th Cir.) (*Voest-Alpine*), cert. denied, 525 U.S. 1041 (1988)

"*Id.* at" and "*ibid.*" are not to be used when there is an intervening citation (see Rule 4.1).

---

[2] There is one narrow exception to this rule.   An attorney may have used a citation that is unusually lengthy in a footnote, but he or she does not want to repeat the full citation the first time it is used in the text (*e.g.*, a case with a complex, extended history).   In such instances, these examples can be followed:

> See *Jones* v. *United States*, *supra* p. 2 n.4, 697 F.2d at 1197.

> See *Hearings*, *supra* p.5 n.7, at 16.

10.1 Basic Citation Forms

For cases that are part of the case history (cases below of the case in the brief) and are not found in the petition appendix, the name of the case and the court and year parenthetical are omitted the first time the case is cited. For example, citing a case in its *entirety* (in the *Lara-Ruiz* v. *United States* brief in opposition):

681 F.3d 914.

NOT:

United States v. *Lara-Ruiz*, 681 F.3d 914 (8th Cir. 2012).

For subsequent citations to that case, omit the case name. For example, citing a specific page in that case:

681 F.3d at 924.

10.2 Case Names

10.2.1(a) Actions and Parties Cited

Identifying phrases and party names that appear in the official caption should be appended in parentheses *after* the formal case name, but before the citation.

Alternative designations assigned by OSG should be appended in a parenthetical following the citation:

Angelo v. *United States*, [citation] (*Angelo II*).

Area Rate Proceedings (Opinion No. 468), [citation].

Hart v. *Roth (In re Campisano)*, [citation].

ILGWU v. *NLRB (Bernhard-Altmann Texas Corp.)*, [citation].

National Coal. for Pub. Educ. & Religious Liberty (PEARL) [acronym for party's name] v. *Harris*, [citation].

Bankruptcy cases and similar cases will follow Bluebook Rule 10.2.1(a) but is reiterated here: The case name might contain both an adversary and a nonadversary name. If both appear at the beginning of the opinion, cite the adversary name first, followed by the nonadversary name in parentheses. If only one name appears at the beginning of the opinion, then use that name. For example:

> *In re Payne*, 431 F.3d 1055 (7th Cir. 2005). [*Note*: The case name in the original is ONLY *In re Payne*.]

> *United States* v. *Hatton (In re Hatton)*, 220 F.3d 1057 (9th Cir. 2000). [*Note*: The case name in the original is both *In re Hatton* AND *United States v. Hatton*.]

However, if there is a word count issue, the attorney has the discretion to only use the "In re" case name when there are two case names, but the full citation is listed in the TOA.

Some case names have become part of phrases, *e.g.*, *Miranda* warning, and are not to be changed to include a full citation for the case name, *e.g.*, warning under *Miranda v. Arizona*, 384 U.S. 436 (1966).

10.2.1(b) Procedural Phrases

Despite Rule 10.2.1(b), we will generally omit "*ex rel.*" and the name of the relator when including that information is cumbersome and unnecessary. Thus, use *Block* v. *North Dakota*, 461 U.S. 273 (1983), not *Block* v. *North Dakota ex rel. Board of Univ. & Sch. Lands*, 461 U.S. 273 (1983). This rule does not mean that *ex rel.* should always be eliminated; some cases are well known by a name that includes *ex rel.* (*e.g.*, *United States ex rel. Marcus* v. *Hess*, 317 U.S. 537 (1943)). Generally, the attorney has discretion whether or not to include *ex rel.*, and that choice should not be altered by the paralegals.

10.2.1(c) Abbreviations

Paralegals routinely abbreviate case names in citations. However, it is ultimately the attorney's decision whether or not to abbreviate words in case names. When a word in a case name is abbreviated, the abbreviations listed in Bluebook T6, 430-431 will govern.

There are four exceptions to this rule. First, paralegals will abbreviate words to achieve consistency throughout a brief. Once a word in a case name has been abbreviated, that same word is to be abbreviated wherever it appears in any case citation (unless it is the first word in a party's name, including the first word after *In re* or *Ex rel.*).

Second, there are several words that will *always* appear as abbreviations in case names: &, Ass'n, Bros., Co., Corp., Inc., Int'l, Ltd., and No. For additional rules pertaining to abbreviation of case names, see Rule 10.2.

Third, when case names are used in text (in sentences), abbreviations will not be used, except for &, Ass'n, Bros., Co., Corp., Inc., Int'l, Ltd., and No.

Fourth, do not abbreviate the first words of a party's name, including the first word after *In re* or *Ex rel.*

To determine whether to use United States or U.S. with a federal agency name in a case name depends on how the case name appears in the original.

For example:

American Mining Cong. v. United States EPA, 965 F.2d 759 (9th Cir. 1992).

[*Note*: The case name appears in the original as United States Environmental Protection Agency. It is the attorney's discretion whether to abbreviate the federal agency name.]

NRDC, Inc. v. *U.S. EPA*, 656 F.2d 768 (D.C. Cir. 1981).

[*Note*: The case name appears in the original as U.S. Environmental Protection Agency. It is the attorney's discretion whether to abbreviate the federal agency name.]

10.2.1(f) Geographical Terms

Rule 10.2.1(f), which prohibits the use of "State of," "Commonwealth of," and "People of" in case citations except when citing decisions of the courts of that particular State, is limited to cases where the proper name of a party includes one of those three descriptive terms. In those situations, the prepositional phrase "of * * * " is omitted. Thus, where the Commonwealth of Pennsylvania is a party in a Pennsylvania state court, the proper citation would be:

> *Commonwealth* v. *Thomas*, 506 A.2d 420 (Pa. Super. Ct. 1986).

BUT:

> *Abu-Jamal* v. *Pennsylvania*, 555 U.S. 916 (2008).

In Virgin Islands cases, we will follow the common practice of using "Government of the Virgin Islands," rather than eliminating "Government of." Thus: *Government of the Virgin Islands* v. *Hoheb*, 777 F.2d 138 (3d Cir. 1985).

However, where a party to the litigation is a city or other governmental entity of lesser consequence than a State (*e.g.*, City of, Town of, County of, Village of, Township of, or Hamlet of), the descriptive term is omitted unless the expression *begins* a party name. Accordingly, in cases in which New York is a party, regardless of the court the action is being prosecuted in, the proper citation would be:

> *Clinton* v. *City of New York*, 524 U.S. 417 (1998).

Omit prepositional phrases of location not following "City" or similar expressions, unless the omission would leave only one word in the name of the party, or unless the name of the party is a corporate name. Include designations of national or larger geographical areas (*Note*: *state* geographical areas are smaller than national geographical areas), except in union names, but omit "of America" after "United States." For example:

> *Kiley* v. *First Nat'l Bank*

Wilder v. *City of Richmond*

Smilecare Dental Grp. v. *Delta Dental Plan of Cal., Inc.*
[state is part of incorporated name]

NOT:

Kiley v. *First Nat'l Bank of Maryland*

Wilder v. *City of Richmond, Virginia*

Smilecare Dental Grp. v. *Delta Dental Plan*

Be aware that in some cultures, a person's "last" name may comprise more than one word. For example:

Alvarez-Alvarez v. *United States*

Garcia y Garcia v. *United States*

10.2.1(j) Commissioner of Internal Revenue

Cite as "Commissioner" in citations. For example:

Allen v. *Commissioner*, 925 F.2d 348 (9th Cir. 1991).

NOT:

Allen v. *Commissioner of Internal Revenue*, 925 F.2d 348 (9th Cir. 1991).

10.3   Reporters and Other Sources

10.3.1 Parallel Citations and Which Source(s) to Cite

Generally, parallel citations will be avoided.

For cases not yet appearing in the United States Reports, cite the Supreme Court Reporter, but avoid reference to the Lawyers' Edition and United States Law Week. For cases not yet appearing in the Supreme Court Reporter, cite the slip opinion. Parallel citations for state court cases are not required. Citations to an official state reporter should be made only where there is no parallel citation to the regional reporter.

10.4 Court and Jurisdiction

Although Rule 10.4 generally provides that "[e]very case citation must indicate which court decided the case," this rule is altered when the surrounding text clearly indicates which court authored the cited opinion:

> The Second Circuit recently held * * * . *British Am. Commodity Options Corp.* v. *Bagley*, 552 F.2d 482 (1977).

> [*Note*: Because Second Circuit is textual, "2d Cir." is omitted in the parenthetical.]

BUT:

> At least one court has held * * * . *British Am. Commodity Options Corp.* v. *Bagley*, 552 F.2d 482 (2d Cir. 1977).

If there are several dispositions within a single case by the same court, the court designation needs to be repeated (see example in Rule 10.7.1(a)). For example:

> *Mata* v. *Johnson*, 99 F.3d 1261 (5th Cir. 1996), vacated in part on reh'g, No. 96-20218, 1997 WL 27052 (5th Cir. Jan. 23, 1997).

NOT:

> *Mata* v. *Johnson*, 99 F.3d 1261 (1996), vacated in part on reh'g, No. 96-20218, 1997 WL 27052 (5th Cir. Jan. 23, 1997).

10.4(a) Federal Courts

In indicating the court of appeals circuit in a case citation's parenthetical, we will follow the Bluebook and refer to "2d" and "3d" rather than "2nd" and "3rd."

10.4(b) State Courts

When citing state court decisions in regional reporters, include the state name in the court parenthetical even if it duplicates information provided elsewhere within the citation (*e.g., Jones* v. *Smith*, 540 P.2d (Mo. Ct. App. 1987), aff'd, 542 P.2d 1 (Mo. 1988)).

10.5   Date or Year

It is not necessary to include a date in the case citation if the surrounding text clearly indicates the date:

> In 1977, the Second Circuit held * * * . *British Am. Commodity Options Corp.* v. *Bagley*, 552 F.2d 482.

NOT:

> In 1977, the Second Circuit held * * * . *British Am. Commodity Options Corp.* v. *Bagley*, 552 F.2d 482 (2d Cir. 1977).

If there are several dispositions within a single case in the same year, include the year only for the last disposition in that year. For example:

> *Grimmett* v. *Brown*, 75 F.3d 506 (9th Cir.), cert. granted, 116 S. Ct. 2512 (1996), cert. dismissed, 117 S. Ct. 759 (1997).

NOT:

> *Grimmett* v. *Brown*, 75 F.3d 506 (9th Cir. 1996), cert. granted, 116 S. Ct. 2512 (1996), cert. dismissed, 117 S. Ct. 759 (1997).

Nineteenth-century Supreme Court opinions (from 2 Dall. through 107 U.S.) are often misdated in the United States Reports. *See* http://www.supremecourt.gov/opinions/datesof-decisions.pdf.

10.5(c) Pending Cases and Cases Dismissed Without Opinion

Dates of significant activity in pending cases (*e.g.*, filings, arguments, argument scheduled, etc.) can be noted in parentheticals following the case citation. For example:

For a case in which a certiorari petition or jurisdictional statement has been filed but not acted on:

Smith v. *Prisco*, petition for cert. pending, No. 88-1039 (filed Nov. 10, 1988).

US Airways, Inc. v. *Sabre Holding Corp.*, appeal pending, No. 17-960 (3d Cir. filed Apr. 5, 2017).

For a case in which a petition for a writ of certiorari has been granted or probable jurisdiction noted, but that has not yet been argued:

Browning Ferris Indus. v. *Kelco Disposal, Inc.*, cert. granted, No. 88-556 (Dec. 5, 1988).

United States v. *Halper*, probable jurisdiction noted, No. 87-1383 (June 3, 1988).

For a case in which argument has been scheduled:

Suitam v. *Tahoe Reg'l Planning*, cert. granted, No. 96-243 (oral argument scheduled for Feb. 26, 1997).

For an argued case awaiting decision:

Mesa v. *California*, No. 87-1206 (argued Dec. 6, 1988).

Jones v. *Smith*, No. 95-12345 (9th Cir. argued June 1, 1996).

For a case that was argued twice and awaiting decision:

Sessions v. *Dimaya*, No. 15-1498 (reargued Oct. 2, 2017)

Cases with pending decisions are not listed in the TOA. If an opinion is cited from a case with subsequent history that is still pending, the case *is* included in the TOA, along with the appropriate subsequent history of that opinion. For appropriate explanatory phrases of subsequent history, see Bluebook T8, at 434-435.

In citing pending or unreported cases with multiple parties or numbers, only cite the docket number pertaining to the case name listed in the caption; never use "*et al.,*" "*et seq.,*" or "etc." to refer to the other parties or numbers. For example:

Shelley v. *Kraemer*, No. 83-592.

NOT:

Shelley v. *Kraemer*, *et al.*, Nos. 83-592 & 83-677.

Shelley v. *Kraemer*, Nos. 83-592 *et al.*

10.6   Parenthetical Information Regarding Cases

Parenthetical information about a case should follow directly after the citation for that case, before any citation for prior or subsequent history.

Plurality opinions, as well as other opinions that are not the single, clear holding of the majority, must be indicated parenthetically. For a Supreme Court decision, if the top of the page of the United States Reports is annotated "Opinion of XXXX, J.," there is a very good possibility that this is a plurality opinion.[3]

Unless already indicated textually, we will always include the following parenthetical information, if applicable:

(plurality opinion) [for plurality opinions]

(XXXX, J., concurring)

(XXXX, J., concurring in the judgment)

---

[3] The attached guidelines (Attachment 1, *infra*, p. 83) supplied by the Reporter of Decisions of the Supreme Court, should be used in determining if an opinion is a plurality opinion.

(XXXX, J., dissenting)

(XXXX, J., concurring in part and dissenting in part)

(XXXX, J., in chambers)

NOT: (XXXX, J., Circuit Justice)

(joint opinion of XXXX and XXXX, JJ.)

(per curiam) [for Supreme Court decisions; use of "per curiam" is discretionary for all other courts]

An opinion in a decision in which the result is unclear or complicated (*e.g.*, concurring in part and concurring in part in the result) may be cited as it is noted at the top of the page of the United States Reports to conserve space or minimize word count. (This form should only be used where necessary and not as a replacement for the above-mentioned forms). Thus:

(opinion of XXXX, J.)

10.7 Prior and Subsequent History

Denials of certiorari by the Supreme Court should usually be noted; however, we generally do not note when the Court denies rehearing.

Subsequent history does not include negative indirect history (*e.g.*, superseded by statute as stated in, disapproved of by, etc.); however, paralegals should bring relevant indirect negative history to the attention of the assistant revising the brief.

For further information on how to structure case histories, see Rule 1.5.

It is our practice to list denials of writs of certiorari when an attorney is referencing petitions for writs of certiorari being denied in prior cases for the same issue as the present case in the following manner:

This Court has recently and repeatedly denied petitions for writs of certiorari challenging sentences in cases in which district courts relied on acquitted conduct to compute defendants' advisory Sentencing Guidelines ranges. See, *e.g.*, *Siegelman* v. *United States*, 136 S. Ct. 798 (2016) (No. 15-353); *Roman-Oliver* v. *United States*, 135 S. Ct. 753 (2014) (No. 14-5431); *Ciavarella* v. *United States*, 134 S. Ct. 1491 (2014) (No. 13-7103); *Kokenis* v. *United States*, 132 S. Ct. 2713 (2012) (No. 11-1042); *Magluta* v. *United States*, 556 U.S. 1207 (2009) (No. 08-731); *Morris* v. *United States*, 553 U.S. 1065 (2008) (No. 07-1094); *Edwards* v. *United States*, 549 U.S. 1283 (2007) (No. 06-8430).

Note that a paralegal must check the following: (1) the case citation; (2) the Supreme Court docket number; and (3) the issue of the prior cases, which can be found by looking at the issue found in the government's brief in opposition for that case.

10.7.1 Explanatory Phrases and Weight of Authority

Do not italicize words and abbreviations used to describe the history of a given case (*e.g.*, cert. denied, aff'd, and rev'd).

If a cited case is being reversed on other grounds, this fact should be indicated in the explanatory phrase.

10.7.1(d) Multiple Dispositions

Often, there will be multiple dispositions by the same court for the same case. See the following "fictional" examples:

Jones v. *Smith*, 100 F.3d XXX (5th Cir.), **cert. denied, 502 U.S. 226, and 502 U.S. 227 (1992).** [multiple denials of cert. in the same year and same volume of U.S.]

Jones v. *Smith*, 100 F.3d XXX (5th Cir.), **cert. denied, 502 U.S. 226 (1992).** [denial of cert. in the same year]

Jones v. *Smith*, 100 F.3d XXX (5th Cir.), **cert. denied, 502 U.S. 226, 502 U.S. 238, and 503 U.S. 300 (1992).** [multiple denials of cert. in the same year but in different volumes of U.S.]

United States v. *Maddox*, 944 F.2d 122 (6th Cir.), **cert. denied, 502 U.S. 950, and 502 U.S. 992 (1991), 502 U.S. 1063, 502 U.S. 1113, 504 U.S. 924, and 504 U.S. 961 (1992), and 501 U.S. 1206 (1994).** [multiple denials of cert. in the same and different years, and in the same and different volumes of U.S.]

Jones v. *Smith*, 100 F.3d XXX (5th Cir.), **cert. denied, 502 U.S. 226, and cert. dismissed, 503 U.S. 300 (1992).** [denial of cert. and dismissal of cert. in same year]

Jones v. *Smith*, 100 F.3d XXX (5th Cir.), **cert. denied, 502 U.S. 226 (1992), aff'd, 505 U.S. 200 (1993).** [denial of cert., then subsequent affirmance, in different years]

10.7.2   Different Case Name on Appeal

The use of *sub nom.* is governed by Rule 10.7.2. This rule provides (emphases added):

> When the name of the case differs in [prior or] subsequent history, the new name must be given[.] * * * Do not provide a [new] case name[, however,] (i) when the parties' names are merely reversed; (ii) when the citation in which the difference occurs is to a *denial of certiorari or rehearing*[, or] (iii) when, in the appeal of an administrative action, the name of the *private party* remains the same[.]

When the name of the administrative officer of an administrative agency changes, this is merely a change in the name of the public party and would not warrant the use of *sub nom.* to indicate the change of name under this rule.

10.8   Special Citation Forms

10.8.1   Pending and Unreported Cases

10.8.1(a) Cases Available on Electronic Media

It is preferred that parallel citations to electronic databases be included when citing *non-Supreme Court* slip opinions. For decisions that are unpublished or yet to be reported, an electronic database citation, if available, should be included. For example:

> *Smith* v. *Ashcroft*, No. 02-7079, 2003 WL 21206 (9th Cir. May 20, 2003), **slip op. 3.** [slip op. citation]

> *Smith* v. *Ashcroft*, No. 02-7079, **2003 WL 21206, at *3** (9th Cir. May 20, 2003). [electronic form citation]

> *Tate* v. *Clover*, No. 02-1444, **2003 WL 92222 (D. Md. May 1, 2003) (241 F. Supp. 2d 699).** [by attorney request only]

For more information concerning electronic media citations, see Rule 10.8.1(a).

10.8.1(b) Cases Available in Slip Opinions

We will follow the Bluebook in citing slip opinions with several exceptions: (1) we will continue to place the *slip opinion* page citation (but not the database page citation) after the date; (2) we will omit the word "at" when giving slip opinion page citations (but not when giving electronic database page citations) in both full *and* short citations; (3) the electronic database citation may be included, if available; and (4) page citations can be to either the slip opinion or the electronic database, but not both. Furthermore, the choice of citation (database or slip opinion) should be consistent throughout the brief. A typical *Supreme Court* citation will read as follows:

> *Babbitt* v. *Youpee*, No. 95-1595 (Jan. 21, 1997), slip op. 3. [standard citation style]

BUT [if attorney requires electronic citations]:

> *Babbitt* v. *Youpee*, No. 95-1595, 1997 WL 17839, at *3-*4 (Jan. 21, 1997). [must include electronic page number]

For *non-Supreme Court* slip opinions, use the same format but indicate the court in the parenthetical before the date:

> *Clark* v. *Homrighous*, No. CIV.A.90-1380-T, 1991 WL 55402, at *3 (**D. Kan.** Apr. 10, 1991).

In citing a recent certiorari denial that is not yet in the Supreme Court Reporter, use the following format:

Tyrues v. *Shinseki*, cert. denied, No. 13-813 (Apr. 7, 2014).

In citing an unreported *original* case, use the following style:

Maine v. *New York*, **No. 94, Orig.** (May 15, 1985).

In citing pending or unreported cases with multiple parties or numbers, only cite the docket number pertaining to the case name listed in the caption; never use "*et al.*," "*et seq.*," or "etc." to refer to the other parties or numbers.   For example:

Shelley v. *Kraemer*, **No. 83-592**

NOT:

Shelley v. *Kraemer et al.*, **Nos. 83-592 & 83-677**

Shelley v. *Kraemer*, **Nos. 83-592 *et al.***

When citing slip opinions, follow the Court's own style in case numbering, but abbreviate "civil" and "criminal" as follows:

Jones v. *United States*, **No. 77 Civ. 1782**

Smith v. *United States*, **Crim. No. 84-1339**

NOT:

Jones v. *United States*, **No. 77 Civil Action 1782**

Smith v. *United States*, **Criminal No. 84-1339**

In citations, abbreviate case number information wherever possible and eliminate unnecessary words.

When citing slip opinions, follow the court's own style in case numbering.   However, if there is a number followed by a colon in the beginning of the case number in district court cases, the number followed by a colon will be dropped. For example:

No. 13-cv-1874

NOT:

No. 3:13-cv-1874

In addition, omit extra zeros in case numbers, escept the zero in the year. For example:

No. 03-cv-845

NOT:

No. 03-cv-00845

See Rule 10.5(c) for further instructions on how to cite pending cases.

10.8.1(c) Other pending and Unreported Cases

A case published in the Federal Appendix is considered to be an unreported opinion.

10.8.2 Fifth Circuit Split

We will not cite Fifth Circuit decisions rendered in 1981 by month, nor will we distinguish between Units A and B of the former Fifth Circuit.

10.8.3 Briefs, Court Filings, and Transcripts

Citations to court filings (unlike textual references to court filings) are abbreviated. Thus: J.S. (jurisdictional statement), Mot. to Affirm (motion to affirm), Pet. (petition), or Br. in Opp. (brief in opposition). Use "Pet. Br." and "Resp. Br." to refer to briefs for non-government parties, "Gov't Br." to refer to briefs on behalf of federal officials or agencies, and "U.S. Br." to refer to briefs for the United States. Spell out "Appellant's," "Appellee's," and "Reply" as well as other identifying adjectives that would create confusion if abbreviated.

In general, any pleading filed in the court of appeals can be cited by adding C.A. to the appropriate abbreviation (*e.g.*, Jones C.A. Br., Resp. C.A. Br., or Pet. C.A. Br.). To prevent confusion when citing briefs for the United States filed in courts of appeals, avoid the form "U.S. C.A. Br." and use instead "Gov't C.A. Br." No footnoted explanations are necessary for any of these conventions.

The first time Administrative Record or Presentence Investigation Report is cited, the full name needs to be provided followed by (A.R.) or (PSR) whether it is cited textually or as a citation the first time. For example:

> The Presentence Investigation Report (PSR) states * * * . PSR ¶ 15.

> Presentence Investigation Report (PSR) ¶ 2.

Judgment will be spelled out when appearing alone, but abbreviated when it is used as Summary J.

For common named court documents, *e.g.*, Judgment, Gov't C.A. Br., no date is provided in a parenthetical if there is only one document. If there are, for example, multiple judgments, a date would be provided as: 1/21/15 Judgment, as is done for transcripts. If there are multiple, for example, government court of appeal briefs in multiple dockets, the lower-court case number would be used, *e.g.*, 15-222 Gov't C.A. Br. If there is more than one, for example, government court of appeal brief filed within the same docket, then a date will be used, *e.g.*, 1/21/15 Gov't C.A. Br.

Use "App." to refer to an appendix that is bound together with the document or filing that it accompanies (*e.g.*, Pet. App.). When there is more than one appendix or when there are citations to appendices from the Fifth, Sixth, Ninth, or Eleventh Circuits, follow the following examples:

> Appellant's App.

Appellee's App.

Gov't C.A. App.   [United States appendix or appendix for an agency]

83-1844 C.A. App.   [multiple case number appendix]

Jones C.A. App.   [multiple party appendix]

C.A. E.R.   [Excerpts of Record, Ninth Circuit]

C.A. R.E.   [Record Excerpts, Fifth and Eleventh Circuits]

C.A. ROA.   [Record on Appeal, Fifth and Sixth Circuits]

When a brief contains multiple appendices, do not cite a specific appendix (*e.g.*, J.S. App. A, Pet. App. D) except in unusual circumstances (*e.g.*, for multiple appendices that are separately numbered, citation to a specific appendix is necessary).   As long as the appendix pages are consecutively or distinctively numbered, it is accurate and helpful to the reader to cite the range of specific page numbers when referring to a particular appendix.   Thus:

The court of appeals affirmed.   Pet. App. 1a-45a.

NOT:

The court of appeals affirmed.   Pet. App. A.

BUT for separately paginated appendices:

The court of appeals affirmed.   Pet. App. A1-A45.

Use the form "App., *infra*, 1a-5a" or "App., *infra*" when referring to an appendix *bound together* with the brief in which the citation appears.

When citing particular pages in the record or transcript, use the abbreviation "R." or "Tr."   The default is to cite a transcript as "Tr.," but an attorney has the discretion to cite it as a "Tr." or as a district court document.   When a multivolume record or a multivolume transcript is not paginated consecutively, use one of the following forms to refer to particular transcript or record pages.

5 Tr. 322.

4 R. 68.

Exhibits are cited as "Ex.," "U.S. Ex.," "GX," "PX," or "DX."

It often will not be sufficient to use one of the above conventions without supplying additional information when citing court filings. Examples of such situations are citations to court documents filed in consolidated cases or cases in which multiple petitions or amicus briefs have been filed. In such situations, place additional identifying information before the abbreviated name of the court filing. For example:

77-1401 Pet. 23-29. [docket number]

Smith Pet. 14. [petitioner's name]

Jones J.S. App. 15a. [appellant's or appellee's name]

ACLU Amicus Br. [name of amicus]

When introducing page references in citations to court documents *related to the instant case* at any level, do not use "at" (*e.g.*, Pet. 5; Br. in Opp. 14; J.S. 12; Gov't C.A. Br. 3; Mem. of Points and Authorities 9). Occasionally, authors will cite court filings that are not part of the *instant* case. These citations differ from the citations to court filings in the instant case in several ways: They should (a) include "at" after the abbreviated court filing title and before the page number, (b) include a case citation after the cited source, and (c) parenthetically include the docket number if the opinion has been reported. For example:

Gov't Br. at 9, *Polsby* v. *Shalala*, 113 S. Ct. 1940 (1993) (No. 92-966).

U.S. Br. at 9, *United States* v. *MacDonald*, No. 80-1582 (Mar. 31, 1982).

As discussed in our brief (at 9), *Polsby* v. *Shalala*, 113
S. Ct. 1940 (1993) (No. 92-966), * * * .

For subsequent citations to court documents not related to
the instant case, "*supra*" can be used in place of the case citation:

Gov't Br. at 10, *Polsby*, *supra* (No. 92-966).

No footnoted explanations are necessary for any of these conventions.   For capitalization of citations to court documents,
see Bluepages B7.3.   For more information concerning citations to court filings, see Rule 8.   For information on how to
structure the citation, see Rule 1.

10.9   Short Forms for Cases

As discussed in Rule 4.2(a), generally "*supra*" is not used to
refer to cases previously cited.   However, "*supra*" will be
used when citing the case name without page citation.   An
entire case may be cited with the use of "*supra*" (*e.g.*, *Wuchter*
v. *Pizzutti*, *supra*), but "*supra*" may also be used with an established short form for a case name.   For example, *Valley
Forge*, *supra*, could be used in place of *Valley Forge Christian College* v. *Americans United for Separation of Church
and State, Inc.*, *supra*.

It is an attorney's discretion whether to use a short form for
cases.   If a short form is used, it is the attorney's discretion
as to whether it appears with the full citation for the first time
in the statement, summary of argument, or argument/discus-
sion sections.

A short form of citation can include either one or both parties
in the caption, as Rule 10.9 indicates.   Thus, both *United
States* v. *Calandra*, 414 U.S. at 343, and *Calandra*, 414 U.S.
at 343, are good short forms.

Even when a short form for a case name adopts the first word
or words of a party's name, the short form should still be formally established with a parenthetical; however, this estab-
lishment is an attorney's discretion.   The location of the

short form would appear after the citation and before any subsequent history. Thus:

Voest-Alpine Trading USA Corp. v. *Bank of China*, 142 F.3d 887, 890 (5th Cir.) (*Voest-Alpine*), cert. denied, 525 U.S. 1041 (1988).

Short citations to slip opinions (as opposed to electronic databases) do not use the word "at" before the page citation. For example:

Carlucci, slip op. 10. [slip opinion]

BUT:

Clark, 1991 WL 5088, at *2. [electronic database]

Constitutions, Statutes, and Legislative, Administrative, and Executive Materials

11   Constitutions

As discussed in Rule 8, references to part of a constitution (federal, state, or foreign) will be capitalized in both text *and citations*. In text, refer to the "Fifth Amendment" and "Article III." Follow Bluebook Rule 11 in structuring citations to constitutions (*e.g.*, U.S. Const. Amend. XIV, § 2).

In accordance with Rule 11, there is no comma dividing "U.S. Const." and the first subdivision in the citation. Thus:

U.S. Const. Art. I, § 9.

NOT:

U.S. Const., Art. I, § 9.

12   Statutes

12.3   Current Official and Unofficial Codes

For federal statutes, cite only the United States Code and not unofficial codes (U.S.C.A. or U.S.C.S.). If the relevant statute is not in the United States Code, cite the Statutes at Large.

For example:

> Passenger Rail Investment and Improvement Act of 2008, Pub. L. No. 110-432, Div. B, 122 Stat. 4907.

BUT:

> Passenger Rail Investment and Improvement Act of 2008, Pub. L. No. 110-432, Div. B, Tit. II, § 207, 122 Stat. 4916 (49 U.S.C. 24101 note).

For example:

> Individuals with Disabilities Education Improvement Act of 2004, Pub. L. No. 108-446, 118 Stat. 2647.

NOT:

> Individuals with Disabilities Education Improvement Act of 2004, 20 U.S.C. 1400 note.

Statutes in the United States Code will be cited without section symbols (§). We will, however, continue to use section symbols in citations to the Statutes at Large, state session laws, and state codes that themselves use the symbol.

If a named federal act is found in the Statutes at Large and is part of a larger named federal act, then information, *e.g.*, Div., Tit., Subtit., must be provided for clarity and accuracy. Refer to the Popular Names of the United States Code for guidance on citing these named federal acts.

For example:

> Omnibus Consolidated Appropriations Act, 1997, Pub. L. No. 104-208, 110 Stat. 3009.

> Treasury, Postal Service, and General Government Appropriations Act, 1997, Pub. L. No. 104-208, Div. A, Tit. I, § 101(f), 110 Stat. 3009-314.

> Treasury Department Appropriations Act, 1997, Pub. L. No. 104-208, Div. A, Tit. I, § 101(f) [Tit. I], 110 Stat. 3009-314.

> Illegal Immigration Reform and Immigrant Responsibility Act of 1996, Pub. L. No. 104-208, Div. C, 110 Stat. 3009-546.

For example:

> Anti-Drug Abuse Act of 1986, Pub. L. No. 99-570, 100 Stat. 3207.

> Career Criminals Amendment Act of 1986, Pub. L. No. 99-570, Tit. I, Subtit. I, 100 Stat. 3207-39.

12.3.1 Additional Information

12.3.1(a) Name and Original Section Number

The first time that a statute is provided in a brief, it should be fully cited.

Federal "Public Laws" before 1957 are cited by "chapter" number; subsequent acts are cited by "Pub. L. No."

Abbreviations and popular or shortened names should be appended in parentheses as follows:

> Federal Pesticide Act of 1978 (1978 Amendments).

> Labor Management Relations (Taft-Hartley) Act.

Longshoremen's and Harbor Worker's Compensation Act (Longshoremen's Act).

Sherman Act (the Act).

Financial Institutions Reform, Recovery, and Enforcement Act of 1989 (FIRREA).

If a short form is created at the attorney's discretion, the location of the short form would be after the statute's name and before the citation.   For example:

Immigration and Nationality Act (INA), 8 U.S.C. 1101 *et seq.*

Immigration and Nationality Act (INA), ch. 477, 66 Stat. 163.

Immigration Act of 1990 (1990 Act), Pub. L. No. 101-649.

12.3.1(e) Supplements

When citing the United States Code, include a date only for clarity or if the cited section derives from a supplement or an edition other than the most recent full edition of the Code. The supplement used is the most current supplement, unless a specific year is needed.   For example:

18 U.S.C. 2.   [example that is found only in main volume of the most recent Code]

52 U.S.C. 10101 (Supp. III 2015).   [example that is found only in a supplement]

29 U.S.C. 794 (2012 & Supp. IV 2016).   [example that is found in both the main volume and a supplement]

When an entire act is cited by the use of "*et seq.*," do not include a date even if portions of the act are contained in more recent supplements.   However, include the date when the entire act can only be found in the supplement.

For example:

Immigration and Nationality Act, 8 U.S.C. 1101 *et seq.*

NOT:

Immigration and Nationality Act, 8 U.S.C. 1101 *et seq.* (2006 & Supp. IV 2016).

BUT:

Voting Rights Act of 1965, 52 U.S.C. 10301 *et seq.* (Supp. III 2015).

When citing material in federal and state statutes, cite pocket parts and bound supplements as "Supp." (Retain all other normal identifying words). For example:

Mo. Ann. Stat. § 514.140 (West Supp. 1984).

NOT:

Mo. Ann. Stat. § 514.140 (West Cum. Pocket Pt. 1984).

12.3.2 Year of Code

United States Code sections will be cited without dates when the statute appears in the most recent full compilation of the United States Code. A citation without a date refers to the most current edition of the United States Code. See Rules 3.1(c) and 12.3.1(e) above about using supplements.

When citing years for state statutes (which we do for *all* such citations, except when state statutes appear in the same paragraph with the same year and the citation form *id.* § ##, is used), include the year and whether the statute appears in a supplement, but not the fact that the supplement is a replacement volume, a revised volume, or a reissued volume. For example:

Ind. Code Ann. § 31-1-7-3 (Michie 1980).

S.D. Codified Laws Ann. § 5-11-6 (Michie 1980).

Neb. Rev. Stat. § 33-116 (1978).

NOT:

Ind. Code Ann. § 31-1-7-3 (Michie repl. 1980).

S.D. Codified Laws Ann. § 5-11-6 (rev. 1980).

Neb. Rev. Stat. § 33-116 (1943 reissued 1978).

12.4   Session Laws

Sections will be cited with section symbols (§) in citations to the Statutes at Large, state session laws, and state codes that themselves use the symbol.   For example:

Buck Act, ch. 787, § 7, 54 Stat. 1060.

Airline Deregulation Act of 1978, Pub. L. No. 95-504, § 20(d)(1), 92 Stat. 1722.

12.4(a) Name

Append abbreviations, popular names, or shortened names in parentheses as follows:

Federal Pesticide Act of 1978 (1978 Amendments).

Labor Management Relations (Taft-Hartley) Act.

Longshoremen's and Harbor Worker's Compensation Act (Longshoremen's Act).

Sherman Act (the Act).

If a short form is created at the attorney's discretion, the location of the short form would be after the statute's name and before the citation.   For example:

Immigration and Nationality Act (INA), 8 U.S. C. 1101 *et seq.*

Immigration and Nationality Act (INA), ch. 477, 66 Stat. 163.

Immigration Act of 1990 (1990 Act), Pub. L. No. 101-649.

12.4(b) Volume

Despite Bluebook Rule 12.4(b), do not give the page of the Statutes at Large on which an act begins when citing only part of that act:

National Environmental Policy Act of 1969, Pub. L. No. 91-190, **§ 102, 83 Stat. 853-854.**

NOT:

National Environmental Policy Act of 1969, Pub. L. No. 91-190, **§ 102, 83 Stat. 852, 853-854.**

However, when citing an entire act (or treaty), give the first page on which the act or treaty begins. Do not follow that page number with *et seq.* for the reason stated in Rule 3.3(b).

12.4(d) Session Laws Amending Prior Acts

Session laws amending prior acts are often divided into sections within sections; that is, the session law itself is divided into primary sections, and these sections, in turn, contain sections of the amended act. Cite the session law's sections with the abbreviation "sec." and the amended act's sections with the symbol "§":

Labor-Management Relations Act, ch. 120, sec. 101, § 8(a)(3), 61 Stat. 140-141.

If the codification information is known, this information can be included parenthetically ("to be codified at xx U.S.C. xxx"). However, any "to be codified at" parenthetical is not part of the formal citation; it is merely optional supplemental information.

12.4(e) Year or Date

Acts or sections in the Statutes at Large may be cited with or without dates, although *the preference is to cite without a date*. Even if the author's preference is to include dates, omit the date parenthetical when the year of enactment is clear from the name of the statute.

12.4(f) Codification Information

If a cited session-law provision has been codified, give the codified version parenthetically. However, do not indicate that the section is "codified at"; it can be assumed that this is where the provision is codified. If the provision has not yet been codified but the code location is known, it is appropriate to indicate parenthetically "to be codified at."

12.5 Electronic Media and Online Sources

When states and municipalities only publish their official statutes or ordinances online, the online source may be directly cited.

12.7 Invalidation, Repeal, Amendment, and Prior History

12.7.3 Amendment

The Bluebook mandates that subsequent amendments to a statute be noted parenthetically. OSG style does not so mandate, but makes including this information optional.

12.9 Special Citation Forms

12.9.1 Internal Revenue Code

References in text to the Internal Revenue Code will be to 26 U.S.C.; therefore, do not include section symbols (§) when citing Internal Revenue Code sections in the brief. However, include section symbols with citations to the Internal Revenue Code (I.R.C.) in the *table of authorities and give appropriate citations to 26 U.S.C. parenthetically*.

12.9.3 Rules of Evidence and Procedure

The abbreviations in Rule 12.9.3 for rules of evidence and procedure are the appropriate abbreviations to use in citations. In text, rules of evidence and procedure are spelled out. Note that textual references to rules of evidence and procedure are paginated in the table of authorities.

12.9.5 Model Codes, Restatements, Standards, and Sentencing Guidelines

Restatements

The title of the Restatement is *not* italicized. The volume number is *not* used. For example:

Restatement (Second) of Agency § 395.

Sentencing Guidelines

As described in part "B1," *supra*, we will identify these sources in ordinary Roman type (rather than large and small capitals). To cite a specific Sentencing Guidelines section or commentary, cite as follows:

Basic citation style: Sentencing Guidelines § 2F1.1.

Policy Statement: Sentencing Guidelines § 2F1.1, p.s.

Application note: Sentencing Guidelines § 2F1.1, comment. (n.1).

Background: Sentencing Guidelines § 2F1.1, comment. (backg'd.).

Introduction: Sentencing Guidelines Ch. 3, Pt. D, intro. comment.

Appendix to Guidelines: Sentencing Guidelines App. C, Amend. 70 (Nov. 1, 1989). [*Note*: Date is the effective date of the Amendment.]

Supplement to Appendix to Guidelines: Sentencing Guidelines App. C Supp., Amend. 770 (Nov. 1, 2012). [*Note*: Date is the effective date of the Amendment.]

Do not include dates when citing current federal sentencing guidelines.

12.10   Short Forms for Statutes

Citations to the United States Code will always be full citations unless "*ibid.*" would be appropriate.   Citations to session laws may be shortened in the following ways:

National Environmental Policy Act (the Act) § 102, 83 Stat. 853-854.

Ibid.

§ 102(a), 83 Stat. 854.

Id. at 855.   [only to be used when there are space limitations]

Section 102 of the Act provides that * * * .   83 Stat. 854. [textual reference]

Act § 103, 83 Stat. 856.   [*Note*:   There is *no* comma after the short form.]

NOT:

§ 102.

Citations to *state code provisions* will be full citations, except where *id.* or *ibid.* would be appropriate.   For example:

Id. § 1701.

Id. § 23, 1895 Fla. Laws 20-21.

13   Legislative Materials

We will continue referring to both the "Congress" and the "Session" despite the Bluebook's preference for referring only to the "Congress."

Italicize titles of books, reports, studies, and legislative documents.   Hearing titles should always be italicized.   Include subject-matter title and bill number(s), if any.   Do not italicize Congress, Session, or year.   Names of authors, if available, should be given, as well as institutional authors.

13.2   Bills and Resolutions

Congressional Record citations will not be given for either enacted *or* unenacted bills.

13.3   Hearings

We will continue referring to both the "Congress" and the "Session" despite the Bluebook's preference for referring only to the "Congress."   The *only* words abbreviated in the title of hearings are Comm. and Subcomm.

For example:

> *Proposed Amendments to the Federal Rules of Criminal Procedure: Hearings Before the Subcomm. on Criminal Justice of the House Comm. on the Judiciary*, 95th Cong., 1st Sess. 93 (1977) (*Hearings*).

Subsequent references use the defined short form with the appropriate page, section, or paragraph (without the word "at" or "*supra*"):

> *Hearings* 95.

13.4　Reports, Documents, and Committee Prints

13.4(a) Numbered Federal Reports and Documents

Despite Rule 13.4, we will not give parallel citations to the United States Code Congressional and Administrative News (U.S.C.C.A.N.).

We will depart from the Bluebook on citations to reports of congressional committees by stating the Congress and Session separately, and by omitting the number of the Congress from the report number, even when the report itself bears a hyphenated number such as "100-592." Also, we will insert "No." before the report number. For example:

S. Rep. No. 592, 100th Cong., **2d Sess. 16** (1988).

NOT:

S. Rep. 100-592, **at 16** (1988).

If a short form is created at the attorney's discretion, the location of the short form would be after the citation. For example:

S. Rep. No. 592, l00th Cong., 2d Sess. 16 (1988) (Senate Report).

Subsequent citations do not use "at" before the page number. For example:

Senate Report 17.

If there is more than one Senate Report or House Report, use the year in the short cite, *e.g.*, 1988 Senate Report 17. However, if there is more than one report in any particular year, include the report number in the short cite.

13.5　Debates

When citing the Congressional Record, use the permanent bound edition, unless a bound edition is not available. To convert a daily edition Congressional Record citation to a bound edition, use HeinOnline "Congressional Record Daily to Bound Locator.

A full cite shall mirror the Bluebook format, but my include additional information at the attorney's discretion. Example:

135 Cong. Rec. 4610 (1989) (statement of Sen. McClure).

Subsequent citations to the same volume are shortened, and may also include a parenthetical, as shown:

135 Cong. Rec. at 4610 (statement of Sen. McClure).

Except where "*id.* at" or "*ibid.*" would be appropriate, a full citation of a *daily edition* of the Congressional Record is necessary:

140 Cong. Rec. S8525 (daily ed. July 12, 1994) (statement of Sen. Warner).

Id. at S8526.

NOT:

140 Cong. Rec. **at S8526** (daily ed. July 12, 1994).

13.6 Separately Bound Legislative Histories

Despite OSG's preference against the use of parallel citations, citations to separately bound legislative histories may be retained when useful:

S. Rep. No. 813, 89th Cong., 1st Sess. 3 (1965), *reprinted in* Subcomm. on Administrative Practice and Procedure, Senate Comm. on the Judiciary, 93d Cong., 2d Sess., *Freedom of Information Act Source Book: Legislative Materials, Cases, Articles* 38 (1974).

14   Administrative and Executive Materials

14.1   Basic Citation Forms

Despite Rule 14.1, when citing the Federal Register, we normally omit the title of the notice or regulation; however, it is the attorney's discretion to provide the title.   If the title is provided, that title will be italicized.   For example:

> *Changes to Implement Inter Partes Review Proceedings,* 77 Fed. Reg. 48,680 (Aug. 14, 2012).

Citations of the *Federal Register* should include *BOTH* the first page on which a document begins and the relevant page. For example:

> 65 Fed. Reg. 70,246, 70,250 (Nov. 21, 2000).

Note that the TOA will only have the citation including the first page on which a document begins, and not the individual pages listed.   The individual pages will be paginated the same way as any other miscellaneous source is paginated.

For example, the citation in the TOA would be for the above example:

> 65 Fed. Reg. 70,246 (Nov. 21, 2000).

The date provided for Fed. Reg. is the full date, not just the year.

For short citations, when neither "*id.* at" nor "*ibid.*" is appropriate, follow this example:

> 55 Fed. Reg. at 36,613.

14.2   Rules, Regulations, and Other Publications

14.2(a) Final Rules and Regulations

Regulations in the C.F.R. will be cited without dates when the regulation in question appears in the most recent full compilation of C.F.R. that contains the relevant title.   Regulations in the C.F.R. will be cited without section symbols (§) except when the C.F.R. section number does not reveal the part in which it is listed.

When citing the Federal Register, use the full date, and use commas to separate groups of three digits in numbers that contain five or more digits. See Rule 6.2. Do not use commas in numbers with four digits or when citing United States House and Senate Bills (*e.g.*, H.R. 12222).

Presidential Papers: Executive Orders, Presidential Proclamations, and Reorganization Plans

As indicated by Bluebook T1 (at 223-224), cite Executive Orders, Presidential Proclamations, and Reorganization Plans according to the version of 3 C.F.R. in which they appear, whenever possible. (This will often require inclusion of the date of the C.F.R. in which the material appears, as these sources appear only once, in the compilation version of the C.F.R. for the year they were ordered or proclaimed.) If the Executive Order is not found in 3 C.F.R. then cite to the Federal Regulation using the full date. Executive Orders that can be found in the C.F.R. or the Federal Register will be cited by reference to only one of those sources and not additionally to reprintings in the United States Code.

For example:

Exec. Order No. 12,250, 3 C.F.R. 298 (1980 comp.).

[*Note*: Include "comp." if on spine of the book.]

Exec. Order No. 13,780, 82 Fed. Reg. 13,209 (Mar. 9, 2017).

Do not cite Executive Orders to U.S.C. except for Executive Orders issued before the C.F.R. came into existence and which are not found in the Statutes at Large. The year is not used when citing to Stat. or U.S.C., unless the U.S.C. is not current and an old main edition or supplement is being used.

Note: The Federal Register began publication on March 14, 1936. The earliest Executive Orders and Proclamations published in 3 C.F .R. are Exec. Order No. 7316 (Mar. 13, 1936) and Proclamation No. 2161 (Mar. 19, 1936). The Office of the Federal Register published, in 1974, a compilation entitled "Proclamations and Executive Orders: Herbert Hoover, March 4, 1929, to March 4, 1933."

Books, Periodical Materials, and Secondary Sources

15   Books, Reports, and Other Nonperiodic Materials

15.1   Author

When citing books, pamphlets, and other nonperiodic materials in the text, we will follow the Bluebook and provide the author's full name.

When there are more than two authors, we will follow the Bluebook and use the first author's name followed by "et al.":

William P. Keeton et al., *Prosser and Keeton on the Law of Torts* § 1, at 2 & n.5 (5th ed. 1984).

When the author is a government agency, the smaller department comes before the larger entity. For example:

Div. of Generic Drugs, Fed. Drug Admin., Policy and Procedure Guide (1989).

15.3   Title

Titles of books are not abbreviated unless the original is abbreviated.

15.8   Special Citation Forms

15.8(b) Star Edition

Although the Bluebook correctly notes that many editions of Blackstone's Commentaries have star paging, it has become quite common to cite the widely available reprint of the first edition (the volumes of which date from 1765 to 1769). The pagination in that edition does not always correspond to the star paging, which was based on later editions. Thus, citations of the first edition should track those for a regular book:

1 William Blackstone, *Commentaries* 91 (1765).

15.8(c) Other Named Works

The Bluebook's special citation form for The Federalist will be followed. Please note, however, that as a general matter, Clinton Rossiter's edition should be disfavored, not simply because it has the wrong title (The Federalist Papers), but also because it was not intended to be a scholarly edition and has therefore "modernized" both spelling and punctuation. More reputable editions include those edited by Jacob E. Cooke (1961); George W. Carey and James McClellan (2001); and J.R. Pole (2005).

15.10   Short Citation Forms

If a short form is created at the attorney's discretion, the location of the short form would be after the citation. For example:

Prosser and Keeton on the Law of Torts § 1, at 2 & n.5 (W. Page Keeton ed., 5th ed. 1984) (Prosser).

Subsequent citations do not use "at" before the page number, except if there is a numbered section. For example:

Prosser § 1, at 2.

15.10.1 Short Forms for Works in Collection

We will generally follow the Bluebook and use "*id.* at" when referring to books, pamphlets, and nonperiodic materials. However, if citing the same page(s) or subdivision(s) in the same source as the immediately preceding authority, use "*ibid.*" (not "*id.*").

Supra.

When using short citations to books, pamphlets, and nonperiodic materials, do not use "*supra.*" An appropriate short form will include the author's last name with the specific page reference. For example:

4 Wigmore § 1302, at 721.

Tribe 1303.

Tribe § 15-1, at 1303.

16 Periodical Materials

16.2 Author

For signed materials appearing in periodicals, give the author's full name. Examples:

Charles Heilbrun & John Resnick, Comment, *Convergences: Law, Literature, and Feminism*, 99 Yale L.J. 1913, 1942 n.122 (1990).

Richard A. Posner, Symposium, *Realism About Judges*, 105 Nw. U. L. Rev. 577, 581 (2011).

16.3 Title

Titles of periodical materials, *i.e.*, journals, are not abbreviated unless the original is abbreviated.

16.6 Newspapers

For newspapers, the original print version must be obtained unless it is only found online. If a newspaper article is found in both print and online versions, use the print version. Note that because the titles may differ between the print and online versions, the text of the article needs to be checked to ensure that it is the same article.

Basic citation for print version:

Ari L. Goodman, *O'Connor Warns Politicians Risk Ex-communication over Abortion*, N.Y. Times, June 15, 1990, at A1.

Basic citation for online only version:

John M. Broder, *Geography Is Dividing Democrats over Energy*, N.Y. Times, Jan. 27, 2009, http://www.nytimes.com/2009/01/27/science/earth/27coal.html.

16.9 Short Citation Forms

If a short form is created at the attorney's discretion, the location of the short form would be after the citation. For example:

Charles Heilbrun & John Resnick, Comment, *Convergences: Law, Literature, and Feminism*, 99 Yale L.J. 1913, 1942 n.122 (1990) (*Convergences*).

Richard A. Posner, Symposium, *Realism About Judges*, 105 Nw. U. L. Rev. 577, 581 (2011) (Posner).

Subsequent citations do not use "at" before the page number. For example:

Convergences 1942.

Posner 581.

16.9(a) *Id.*

We will generally follow the Bluebook Rule and use "*id.* at" for subsequent citations to periodical materials. However, if citing to the same page(s) or subdivision(s) in the same source as the preceding authority, use "*ibid.*" (not "*id.*").

16.9(b) *Supra*

Do not use "*supra*" to refer to a previously cited periodical. An appropriate short form, if a short form is not created as shown above, will include the author's last name or title of the article, the volume number, abbreviated periodical title, and "at" before the page citation.   Thus:

Merrill, 52 U. Chi. L. Rev. at 11.

18   The Internet, Electronic Media, and Other Nonprint Resources

18.2   The Internet

We deviate from the Bluebook and do not use "available at."

When an internet citation has no date, do not put "(last visited date)" in the brief.   However, put "(last visited date)" in the TOA.   The date is the date that the brief is sent to the printer.   For example:

In the brief:

Fed. Bureau of Prisons, U.S. Dep't of Justice, Find an Inmate, https://www.bop.gov/inmateloc/.

In the TOA:

Fed. Bureau of Prisons, U.S. Dep't of Justice, Find an Inmate, https://www.bop.gov/inmateloc/ (last visited Aug. 23, 2017) ....

When the author is a federal agency, it is the attorney's discretion whether the name is abbreviated or spelled out in entirety.   Also note that sometimes the name of the federal agency is abbreviated in the text of the brief; a paralegal needs to ask the attorney whether they want the name of the federal agency abbreviated or spelled out in the TOA.   For example:

Div. of Corp. Fin., Sec. & Exch. Comm'n, *Filing Review Process* (Jan.   19,   2017),   https://www.sec.gov/divisions/corpfin/cffilingreview.htm.

[*Note*:   Attorney's discretion to spell out the federal agency names with the appropriate abbreviations, including the first word.   See Bluebook T6, at 430-431.   Also note that the smaller department comes before the larger entity.]

FBI, Uniform Crime Report: *Law Enforcement Officers Killed and Assaulted, 2014: Officers Feloniously Killed* (2015), https://ucr.fbi.gov/leoka/2014/officers-feloniously-killed/officers-feloniously-killed.pdf.

[*Note*: Attorney's discretion to use "FBI" instead of "Fed. Bureau of Investigation," since it is a well-known abbreviation.]

Titles of miscellaneous sources are not abbreviated unless the original is abbreviated.

20   Foreign Materials

20.3   Cases

20.3.1 Common Law Cases

With respect to the citation of cases from Great Britain, Rule 20.3.1 will be relaxed in the event the library does not have some of the preferred sources.   We will follow the rule to the extent the library's collection permits.

21   International Materials

21.4   Treaties and Other International Agreements

For treaties, follow Bluebook Rule 21.4.   Note that article is *not* capitalized.   For example:

Convention Against Torture and Other Cruel, Inhuman or Degrading Treatment or Punishment, *adopted* Dec. 10, 1984, S. Treaty Doc. No. 20, 100th Cong., 2d Sess. (1988), 1465 U.N.T.S. 85.

Convention on the Recognition and Enforcement of Foreign Arbitral Awards art. III, *done* June 10, 1958, 21 U.S.T. 2519, 330 U.N.T.S. 40.

Definitive Treaty of Peace, U.S.-Gr. Brit., art. IV, Sept. 3, 1783, 8 Stat. 82.

Vienna Convention on Diplomatic Relations, *done* Apr. 18, 1961, 23 U.S.T. 3227, 500 U.N.T.S. 95

In the TOA, articles for treaties will be treated like sections in the Statutes at Large. For example, in the TOA:

Convention on the Service Abroad of Judicial and Extra-judicial Documents in Civil or Commercial Matters, done Nov. 15, 1965, 20. U.S.T. 361, 658 U.N.T.S. 163:

art. 1, 20 U.S.T. 362, 658 U.N.T.S. 165 ....

art. 4, 20 U.S.T. 362, 658 U.N.T.S. 167 ....

For United States treaties, OSG's general rule against the use of parallel citations will be altered. Cite official sources and at least one unofficial source for which a citation is readily available. Example:

Agreement Concerning Payments for Certain Losses Suffered During World War II, U.S.-Fr., Jan. 18, 2001, Temp. State Dep't No. 01-36, 2001, 2001 WL 416465.

If a short form is created at the attorney's discretion, the location of the short form would appear after the name of the treaty. For example:

Convention Against Torture and Other Cruel, Inhuman or Degrading Treatment or Punishment (Convention Against Torture), *adopted* Dec. 10, 1984, S. Treaty Doc. No. 20, 100th Cong., 2d Sess. (1988), 1465 U.N.T.S. 85.

Tables

Table numbers used below correspond to Bluebook tables. Any missing table number means that the corresponding Bluebook table is used without exceptions or modifications.

T1   United States Jurisdictions

T1.1   Federal Judicial and Legislative Materials

Federal—Supreme Court

The first volume of U.S. Reports consists of decision of Pennsylvania courts only, reported by Alexander J. Dallas.   Volume 1 contains no U.S. Supreme Court cases.   Cite Volume 1 of U.S. Reports as 1 Dall. and identify the appropriate Pennsylvania court.

Example:

> *Millar* v. *Hall*, 1 Dall. 229 (Pa. 1778).
>
> *Respubilca* v. *De Longchamps*, 1 Dall. 111 (Pa. Oyer & Terminer 1778).

T6   Case Names and Institutional Authors in Citations

As the Bluebook indicates, this table contains only suggested abbreviations.   Authors may or may not abbreviate words in case names, and paralegals should not change the author's choice; however, when a word is abbreviated, it should be abbreviated consistently throughout the document.

BT1   Court Documents

The following abbreviations can be added to the Table:

Administrative Record   A.R.
[*Note*:   Provide the full name the first time it is cited, *i.e.*, Administrative Record (A.R.).]

Appendix to a petition for a writ of   Pet. App.
certiorari

Appendix/Joint Appendix filed in the court of appeals (unless more than one)	C.A. App.
Brief for nongovernment party	Pet. Br. Resp. Br.
Brief filed by the United States in the court of appeals	Gov't C.A. Br.
Brief in opposition	Br. in Opp.
Brief on behalf of government agency	Gov't Br.
Defendant's Exhibit	DX or Def.['s] Ex.
Docket entries	
By date	01-1862 Docket entry (8th Cir. Apr. 17, 2002)

[*Note*: The court, *e.g.*, "8th Cir.," is deleted when the docket entry involved is from the case below.]

By entry number	97-CR-290-1 Docket entry No. 322 (E.D. Mo. July 30, 1999)

[*Note*: The court, *e.g.*, "E.D. Mo.," is deleted when the docket entry involved is from the case below. If a short form is used at the attorney's discretion, the location would be: 97-CR-299-1 Docket entry No. (Docket entry No.) 322 (E.D. Mo. July 30, 1999).]

Documents (numbered) in original record; original pagination is retained	Doc. 12, at 20

[*Note*: the attorney may also cite the actual documents in the lower courts: D. Ct. Doc. 658, at 4 (June 23, 2009).]

[*Note*: When the date is textual, this would become D. Ct. Doc. 658, at 4.]

Excerpts of Record (9th Cir.)	E.R.
Exhibit	Ex.
Government (Agency's) Brief	Gov't Br.
Government's Exhibit	GX or Gov't Ex.
Joint Appendix	J.A.
Jurisdictional Statement	J.S.
Merits Brief	Br.
Motion to Affirm	Mot. to Affirm
Motion to Dismiss	Mot. to Dismiss
Petition for a Writ of Certiorari	Pet.
Petition for Rehearing	Pet. for Reh'g
Plaintiff's Exhibit	PX or Pl.['s] Ex.

Presentence Investigation Report   PSR
   [*Note:* Provide the full name the first time it is cited,
   i.e., Presentence Investigation Report (PSR).]

Record	R.
Record on Appeal (5th & 6th Cir.)	C.A. ROA
Record Excerpts (5th & 11th Cir.)	C.A. R.E.

Reply Brief	Reply Br.
Reply Brief at the Cert. Stage	Cert. Reply Br.
Reply Brief on the Merits	Merits Reply Br.
Supplemental Brief	Supp. Br.
Transcript	Tr.
United States Brief	U.S. Br.
United States Court of Appeals Brief	Gov't C.A. Br.

Miscellaneous Abbreviations:

Judgment	Judgment
Amended Judgment	Am. Judgment
Summary Judgment	Summary J.
Paragraph	para. or ¶
Plea Transcript	Plea Tr.
Sentencing Transcript	Sent. Tr.
Indictment	Indictment
Plea Agreement	Plea Agreement
Addendum to the Presentence Investigation Report	Addendum to PSR

ATTACHMENT 1

§ 10.4. *References to "plurality," "principal," "lead," and "controlling" opinions in U. S. Supreme Court cases.*

A plurality opinion is an opinion announcing the judgment of the Court in a case in which a majority of the Court agrees in the result but there is no majority agreeing with the rationale by which that result is reached *and* in which there are more Members of the Court agreeing with the rationale in the opinion announcing the judgment than with any other rationale (dissenters are not counted in determining whether there is a plurality). *E. g.*, there was a plurality opinion in *United States* v. *MacCollom*, 426 U. S. 317 (1976), where then-Justice Rehnquist announced the judgment of the Court in an opinion in which The Chief Justice, and Justices Stewart and Powell joined, and Justice Blackmun filed an opinion concurring in the judgment.

The joint opinions of Justices Stewart, Powell, and Stevens, announcing the judgments in the death penalty cases *Gregg* v. *Georgia*, 428 U. S. 153 (1976); *Proffitt* v. *Florida*, 428 U. S. 242 (1976); and *Jurek* v. *Texas*, 428 U. S. 262 (1976), have sometimes been erroneously cited as plurality opinions. Those joint opinions are in fact not plurality opinions, because there were three other Justices who, while concurring in the judgments, agreed on a rationale different from that of the opinions announcing the judgments. The joint opinions of Justices Stewart, Powell, and Stevens announcing the judgments in the other death penalty cases decided at the same time, *Woodson* v. *North Carolina*, 428 U. S. 280 (1976), and *Roberts* v. *Louisiana*, 428 U. S. 325 (1976), are, however, plurality opinions, because only two other Justices, each of whom filed separate statements concurring in the judgments, would have followed a rationale different from the joint opinions in reaching the results. The joint opinions in *Gregg*, *Proffitt*, and *Jurek* should be referred to as joint opinions. See *Estelle* v. *Gamble*, 429 U. S. 97, 102, lines 7–8 (1976).

Under the foregoing rules, only Part IV (pp. 869–879) of the joint opinion of Justices O'Connor, KENNEDY, and Souter in *Planned Parenthood of Southeastern Pa.* v. *Casey*, 505 U. S. 833 (1992), may be cited as the plurality opinion. Parts I, II, III, V–A, V–C, and VI of that opinion (pp. 844–869, 879–880, 887–898, and 901) should be cited as the opinion of the Court. Because four other Justices concurred in the judgment on different rationales as to the matters considered in Parts V–B, V–D, and V–E (pp. 881–887, 899–901), those parts should be referred to as the joint opinion.

Do not use the terms "prevailing opinion" or "pivotal opinion," although the term "principal opinion" may be acceptable (see *Wainwright* v. *Spenkelink*, 442 U. S. 901, 902, penult. line (1979) (Rehnquist, J., dissenting); *Hopper* v. *Evans*, 456 U. S. 605, 611, line 8 (1982)). The term "lead opinion" has been used to refer to an opinion announcing the judgment, no part of which has achieved even plurality status. See *Crawford* v. *Marion County Election Bd.*, 553 U. S. 181 (2008). The term "principal opinion" has been used to refer to an opinion, part of which is a majority opinion and part of which is a plurality opinion, see *Parker* v. *Randolph*, 442 U. S. 62, 77, 78, 80 (1979) (Blackmun, J., concurring in part and concurring in judgment), and to an opinion, part of which is a majority opinion and part of which is a nonplurality opinion, see *Idaho* v. *Coeur d'Alene Tribe of Idaho*, 521 U. S. 261, 288-297 (1997) (O'Connor, J., concurring in part and concurring in judgment).

An extreme example of a case where the opinion announcing the judgment of the Court is not a plurality opinion is *Oregon* v. *Mitchell*, 400 U. S. 112 (1970), where Justice Black announced the judgments in an opinion "expressing his own views of the cases." See also *Bellotti* v. *Baird*, 443 U. S. 622 (1979), for another example of a case where there was no plurality opinion (the opinion announcing the judgment is joined by three Justices, but the opinion concurring in the judgment is also joined by three Justices).

NOTE: Concurring in the judgment and concurring in the result mean the same thing. But do not say "JUSTICE X, concurring" where the Justice does not vote with the majority. Also, consistency should be maintained: Do not say "JUSTICE X, concurring in the judgment" where the opinion concludes: "For the foregoing reasons I concur in the result."

The designation "controlling opinion" has sometimes been applied to the opinion that contains the narrower holding in a case in which there is no majority opinion. See, *e. g.*, *Panetti* v. *Quarterman*, 551 U. S. 930, 949 (2007). The Court has explained: "When a fragmented Court decides a case and no single rationale explaining the result enjoys the assent of five Justices, 'the holding of the Court may be viewed as that position taken by those Members who concurred in the judgments on the narrowest grounds . . . .' *Gregg* v. *Georgia,* 428 U. S. 153, 169, n. 15 (1976) (opinion of Stewart, Powell, and Stevens, JJ.)." *Marks* v. *United States,* 430 U. S. 188, 193 (1977). Such an opinion constitutes "clearly established Federal law," the violation of which may authorize federal habeas relief for a state prisoner under 28 U. S. C. § 2254(d)(1). See *Panetti, supra,* at 949.

OFFICE OF THE SOLICITOR GENERAL
SUPPLEMENT TO THE SUPREME COURT RULES

INTRODUCTION

While the Supreme Court Rules govern the format of briefs filed in the Court, the rules provide only general guidelines. The following rules are intended to supplement the Supreme Court Rules in that they provide detailed information on the format of briefs filed by the Office of the Solicitor General.

A. COVER PAGE

1. Eliminate all punctuation at the end of lines in the counsel listing on the cover and last page of the brief. The typical counsel listing on the cover of a brief will look as follows:

DONALD B. VERRILLI, JR.
Solicitor General
Counsel of Record

STUART F. DELERY
Assistant Attorney General

RICHARD DOE
DAVID DOE
Attorneys

Department of Justice
Washington, D.C. 20530-0001
SupremeCtBriefs@usdoj.gov
(202) 514-2217

When outside agency personnel are listed, the cover page will look as follows:

DONALD B. VERRILLI, JR.
Solicitor General
Counsel of Record

Thomas L. Sansonetti
Assistant Attorney General

Paul D. Clement
Deputy Solicitor General

Austin C. Schlick
Assistant to the Solicitor General

Mary Anne Gibbons
General Counsel

David M. Cohen
Attorney

Lori J. Dym
Attorney
Office of General Counsel
United States Postal Service
Washington, D.C. 20260

Department of Justice
Washington, D.C. 20530-0001
SupremeCtBriefs@usdoj.gov
(202) 514-2217

Note: *Make sure that the two bottom lines align on the cover page when the left side takes up less room than the right side.*

On a reply brief or memorandum, the counsel listing will look as follows:

DONALD B. VERRILLI, JR.
Solicitor General
Counsel of Record

Department of Justice
Washington, D.C. 20530-0001
SupremeCtBriefs@usdoj.gov
(202) 514-2217

96

2.   Cover pages of briefs filed on behalf of military services should use the following format:

DONALD B. VERRILLI, JR.
Solicitor General
Counsel of Record

Norman G. Cooper
Col., JAGC, USA

Gary F. Roberson
Lt. Col., JAGC, USA

Patrick Hewitt
Capt., JAGC, USA
Government Appellate Division
Appellate Government Counsel
United States Army Legal
Services Agency
Falls Church, VA 22041-5013

Department of Justice
Washington, D.C. 20530-0001
SupremeCtBriefs@usdoj.gov
(202) 514-2217

Note: *If there are more personnel listed on the left side, make sure that the Solicitor General's name appears higher than the first name of the personnel on the right side.*

3.   When a single opposition is filed in response to more than one petition, the cover and title pages of the opposition should include appropriate plurals:

ON PETITIONS FOR WRITS OF CERTIORARI
TO THE UNITED STATES COURT OF APPEALS
FOR THE FOURTH CIRCUIT

Note the special circumstances in which there is a direct appeal from a district court:

ON APPEAL FROM THE
UNITED STATES DISTRICT COURT
FOR THE DISTRICT OF COLUMBIA

At the merits stage, the cover and title pages should read:

ON WRIT OF CERTIORARI
TO THE UNITED STATES COURT OF APPEALS
FOR THE FOURTH CIRCUIT

4.   Amicus curiae briefs filed at the petition stage should be entitled:

BRIEF FOR THE UNITED STATES
AS AMICUS CURIAE

5.   Merits briefs as amicus curiae should be entitled either

BRIEF FOR THE UNITED STATES
AS AMICUS CURIAE SUPPORTING PETITIONER

or

BRIEF FOR THE UNITED STATES
AS AMICUS CURIAE SUPPORTING RESPONDENT

In appeals, the brief should support "appellant" or "appellee" rather than "petitioner" or "respondent." In briefs filed at the Court's invitation, omit the phrase "supporting _____."

6.   In cases in which the title of the brief requires more than one line to print, the first line should contain only the words "Brief for" and the name or designation of the client on whose behalf the brief is filed. The second and any subsequent lines should contain all modifying phrases (*e.g.*, in opposition, as respondent supporting petitioner, or as amicus curiae). Thus:

BRIEF FOR THE FEDERAL CROSS-RESPONDENTS
IN OPPOSITION

BRIEF FOR THE UNITED STATES
AS AMICUS CURIAE SUPPORTING PETITIONER

7.   Briefs in opposition filed on behalf of federal agencies may be titled either "Brief for the [name of agency] in Opposition" or "Brief for the Respondent in Opposition," as the author prefers. When there is more than one respondent, it is often useful to use the name of the agency, but the form "Brief for the Federal Respondent in Opposition" will usually suffice. The only hard-and-fast rule in this regard is that the title of the brief must be unambiguous.

8.   The parties' names on the cover and first page of all briefs should be exactly as they appear in the Supreme Court's docket but for the following exceptions:

a. If a State is a party, the words "State of," "Commonwealth of," or "People of" should be inserted in front of the state's name. Thus, *Long* v. *Maryland* should be altered to read *Long* v. *State of Maryland.*

b. When space or word count is at a premium, if three or more names appear on the docket as parties on one side, drop all the names except the first and add "et al." If two names appear on the docket, they should both appear on the brief.

c. Change "United States" to "United States of America" in the caption.

d. "Secretary of Interior" and "Secretary of Treasury" should be changed to "Secretary of the Interior" and "Secretary of the Treasury."

e. Do not use "et ux." or "et vir." Instead, use the names of both parties.

9. Original and multiple case numbers should appear on the cover as follows:

No. 94, Orig.

Nos. 00-393, 00-407, 00-417, and 00-427

Multiple case numbers should be combined on the cover, as shown below:

_____

No. 00-407 and 00-417

_____

In the Supreme Court of the United States

_____

DAVID FICHTENBERG, PETITIONER

v.

FEDERAL COMMUNICATIONS COMMISSION, ET AL.

_____

MICHAEL WORSHAM, PETITIONER

v.

FEDERAL COMMUNICATIONS COMMISSION, ET AL.

_____

*ON PETITIONS FOR WRITS OF CERTIORARI
TO THE UNITED STATES COURT OF APPEALS
FOR THE SECOND CIRCUIT*

_____

BRIEF FOR THE RESPONDENTS IN OPPOSITION

_____

However, the first page of the brief with multiple case numbers would be:

In the Supreme Court of the United States

No. 00-407

DAVID FICHTENBERG, PETITIONER

v.

FEDERAL COMMUNICATIONS COMMISSION, ET AL.

———

No. 00-417

MICHAEL WORSHAM, PETITIONER

v.

FEDERAL COMMUNICATIONS COMMISSION, ET AL.

———

ON PETITIONS FOR WRITS OF CERTIORARI
TO THE UNITED STATES COURT OF APPEALS
FOR THE SECOND CIRCUIT

———

BRIEF FOR THE RESPONDENTS IN OPPOSITION

———

10. Capital cases

On the cover page of a paid brief, "(CAPITAL CASE)" will appear below the parties' names. On the cover page of IFP, "(CAPITAL CASE)" will appear below the parties' names.

Example of cover page for paid brief:

Nos. 16-293 and 16-294

In the Supreme Court of the United States

IN RE SHERMAN LAMONT FIELDS, PETITIONER

(CAPITAL CASE)

Example of cover page for IFP brief:

```
---------------

No. 14-9150

---------------

In the Supreme Court of the United States

---------------

NORRIS G. HOLDER, PETITIONER

v.

UNITED STATES OF AMERICA

(CAPITAL CASE)

---------------
```

On the questions(s) presented page, "CAPITAL CASE" will appear before "Question(s) Presented" for both paid and IFP briefs.

Example:

CAPITAL CASE

QUESTION(S) PRESENTED

B. PARTIES TO THE PROCEEDING

The identification of parties to the proceeding in the court below, as required by Supreme Court Rules 14.1(b) and 24.1(b) (2013 ed.), for petitions and merits briefs for the petitioner, shall be given in a separate heading entitled "Parties to the Proceeding" placed on the page immediately after the "Question(s) Presented." Both rules require the inclusion of

> A list of all parties to the proceeding in the court whose judgment is sought to be reviewed (unless the caption of the case contains the names of all the parties).

The beginning page number for this section (II) will appear in parentheses at the bottom of the page.

C. OPINIONS BELOW

1. Although the Rules of the Supreme Court do not strictly require that we list the opinions below in our briefs in opposition, we will continue to do so.   See OSG Writing Preferences Rule C regarding the use of the phrases "unreported" and "not yet reported" with respect to opinions below.

For decisions that are not published but are printed in the Federal Appendix, follow the appropriate example below (bracketed material is optional and is inserted only at attorney's request):

> The opinion of the court of appeals (Pet. App. 1a-16a) is not published in the Federal Reporter but is reprinted in 27 Fed. Appx. 577[, and is available at 2001 WL 1631432].

The opinion of the district court (Pet. App. 18a-26a) is not published in the Federal Supplement but is available at 2000 WL 89008.

NOTE: We will use the abbreviation "Fed. Appx." for the Federal Appendix (per Michael Dreeben). We will not underline the reporter; *e.g.*, Federal Reporter.

2. Place Pet. App. citations in the "Opinions Below" section of briefs in parentheses. Do not use *id.* or *ibid.* in this section.

3. When citing the published opinions of the lower courts in the "Opinions Below" section, do not include the court name and date in parentheses following the citation. Thus:

> The opinion of the court of appeals (Pet. App. 1a-5a) is reported at 212 F.3d 1296.

NOT:

> The opinion of the court of appeals (Pet. App. 1a-5a) is reported at 212 F.3d 1296 (Fed. Cir. 2000).

D. JURISDICTION

1. Do not refer to petitions for rehearing "en banc" in the jurisdictional section. If the court's disposition of a petition for rehearing en banc is relevant, it should be noted in the "Statement" section. Denial of a timely petition for rehearing should be noted in the "Jurisdiction" section as follows:

> A petition for rehearing was denied on December 30, 1988 (Pet. App. 78a).

A petition for rehearing is timely if filed within 90 days of the court of appeals opinion. Under Supreme Court Rule 13.3, even an untimely petition for rehearing may alter the certiorari deadline if it is "appropriately entertain[ed]" by the lower court.

2. When noting the date on which a petition for a writ of certiorari was filed, parenthetically identify the day of the week if the filing would otherwise have been due on a Sunday or a holiday. Thus: "(Monday)" or "(Tuesday following a holiday)."

3. A petition filed out of time should be noted as follows:

> The petition for a writ of certiorari was not filed until September 21, 1989, and is out of time under Rule 13.1 of the Rules of this Court.

4. If a Justice has extended the deadline for filing a petition for a writ of certiorari, that fact should be noted as follows:

> On November 25, 1983, Justice O'Connor extended the time within which to file a petition for a writ of certiorari to and including December 27, 1983, and the petition was filed on that date.

Multiple extensions should be noted as follows:

> On June 10, 2005, Justice Souter extended the time within which to file a petition for a writ of certiorari to and including July 22, 2005. On July 8, 2005, Justice Souter further extended the time to and including August 19, 2005, and the petition was filed on August 18, 2005.

5. The following example is what *may be* included in the "Jurisdiction" section when it is a *merits* brief:

> The judgment of the court of appeals (Pet. App. 4a) [insert Pet. App. citation only if judgment is a separate document and not just *part* of the C.A. opinion] was entered on March 24, 2003. On June 13, 2003, Justice Thomas extended the time within which to file a petition for a writ of certiorari to and including July 22, 2003, and the petition was filed on that date. The petition for a writ of certiorari was granted on September 30, 2003. The jurisdiction of this Court rests on 28 U.S.C. 1254(1).

Note: At the merits stage, jurisdiction "*rests on* 28 U.S.C. 1254(1)." At the petition stage jurisdiction "*is invoked under* 28 U.S.C. 1254(1)."

E. CONCLUSION

1. Use the following form for the conclusion in a typical brief in opposition:

The petition for a writ of certiorari should be denied.

Respectfully submitted.

Use the following form for a typical memorandum in opposition:

* * * * *

> It is therefore respectfully submitted that the petition for a writ of certiorari should be denied.

2.   The following is the appropriate closing for a reply brief at the petition stage:

* * * * *

> For the foregoing reasons and those stated in the petition for a writ of certiorari, the petition should be granted.

> Respectfully submitted.

3.   The following is the appropriate closing for a reply brief at the merits stage:

> For the foregoing reasons and those stated in our opening brief, the judgment of the court of appeals should be ____.

> Respectfully submitted.

4.   The signature section on the last page will look exactly the same as the counsel listing on the front page of the brief or memorandum, with the following exceptions:

> a.   Delete the lines: *Department of Justice*
> *Washington, D.C. 20530-0001*
> *SupremeCtBriefs@usdoj.gov*
> *(202) 514-2217*

> b.   When an outside agency is involved, delete the geographical location but keep the agency's name.

> c.   Omit *"Counsel of Record"* underneath *"Solicitor General."*

The month and year of filing appear after the signature block. The month is not abbreviated and there is no period after the date.

F. MEMORANDUM FORM

1.   Use the memorandum form only for short oppositions to petitions raising a small number of relatively straightforward issues in cases with simple facts. As a general rule, memoranda in opposition should not exceed 1500 words; if the opposition is more than ten pages long, it must be a brief.

2.   Entitle the main section of a petition for a writ of certiorari "REASONS FOR GRANTING THE PETITION," not "Reasons the Petition Should be Granted" or some other variation. Entitle the main section of an amicus brief filed at the petition stage (or a certiorari-stage response that does not oppose certiorari) "DISCUSSION." (*Note*:   There are generally no headings in memoranda.)

OFFICE OF THE SOLICITOR GENERAL
WRITING PREFERENCES

The following rules are given their own separate "mini-manual" because they do not fall neatly into the Bluebook/OSG Citation Manual format.

A. MISCELLANEOUS ABBREVIATION RULES

1. Identifying abbreviations or information should be appended in parentheses as follows:

> The administrative law judge (ALJ) ruled * * * .

> The Environmental Protection Agency (EPA) is authorized to regulate * * * .

> The LaJolla, Rincin, San Pasqual, Pauma, and Pala Pards Indians (Tribes) were granted * * * .

B. MISCELLANEOUS CAPITALIZATION RULES

1. Do not capitalize references to spring, summer, fall, autumn, or winter.

C. MISCELLANEOUS DEFINITIONS

1. We will not use the phrase "not reported" when referring to opinions that do not appear in a reporter.

   Some court opinions are annotated with "not for publication" or other similar note.   These opinions are considered "unreported."   If an opinion is less than two years old, check to see if it has been reported (occasionally courts issue new instructions on publication or newly amended opinions).   A case in either the federal district court or court of appeals that is more than two years old and not reported is considered "unreported."   This phrase should also be used when referring to very old cases that were never reported.

   The phrase "not yet reported" is used when referring to a slip opinion less than three months old or citing a case in a looseleaf service that will be reported in either the West reporters or elsewhere. The phrase is understood to mean that there is every expectation that the case will be reported. Furthermore, if the slip opinion indicates that the opinion is "not for publication," and there is no indication from West that there will be a reporter citation, the opinion is "unreported," rather than "not yet reported." All decisions that are published are considered "reported." Reported decisions may appear either in full text or in a table. Dispositions that appear in a table are cases without an opinion or a published opinion and are cited per the following example:

> *Benge* v. *Marshall*, 709 F.2d 1499 (6th Cir. 1983) (Tbl.).

In the jurisdiction section of our briefs, when we are referring to a decision that is published only in a table in a reporter, the following convention shall be followed:

> The opinion of the court of appeals is unpublished, but the decision is noted at 709 F.2d 1499 (Tbl.).

In referring to an unpublished opinion where the case listed in a table, see the following example:

> *Herman* v. *Rich Kramer Constr., Inc.*, 163 F.3d 602, 1998 WL 664622, at *1 (8th Cir. 1998) (Tbl.).

D. MISCELLANEOUS GRAMMAR PREFERENCES

1. Use "a," not "an," whenever the following word begins with a consonant sound, including an h or y sound. Thus, "a historical analysis," not "an historical analysis"; "a unanimous Court," *not* "an unanimous Court."

For abbreviations and acronyms, use "a," not "an," whenever the abbreviation or acronym begins with a consonant sound when pronounced in the conventional fashion. For example: "an SEC rule," *not* "a SEC rule" ("SEC" is conventionally pronounced "[es]-E-C," starting with a vowel sound); "an NAACP fundraiser" ("NAACP" is pronounced "[en]-double-A-C-P," starting with a vowel sound); and "a FOIA request" ("FOIA" is conventionally pronounced "foy-ah," starting with a consonant sound, not "[ef]-O-I-A").

2.	Use "attorney's fees" rather than "attorneys' fees," unless the governing statute uses another variant.

3.	Use "case law" rather than "caselaw." See Memorandum from Charles Fried to OSG Attorneys (Oct. 2, 1987) (calling for "total extirpation" of this "barbarism").

4.	When using dates in text, follow the following examples:

September 4, 1996

January 20, 1992

October 1997

NOT:

September 4th, 1996

January 20th, 1992

October, 1997

5.	Do not use "et ux." or "et vir." in the caption of a case or elsewhere. This rule applies even though the Court still uses those archaic phrases in the caption of cases in which both members of a married couple are named parties. Use both names as the party in citation, *e.g.*, "Chantal Sackett and Michael Sackett" (No. 10-1062).

6.	When a phrase functions as an adjective, it should generally be hyphenated, but do not use a hyphen to connect an adverb ending in "ly" to the adjective it modifies. Thus, "wholly owned corporation," *not* "wholly-owned corporation," and "fully allocated costs," *not* "fully-allocated costs." Hyphenating phrases functioning as adjectives is at the attorney's discretion; paralegals should only change hyphenated phrases that are not used as adjectives. In addition, paralegals should make sure hyphenated words are hyphenated consistently throughout the brief.

As a general rule, do not use hyphens in words commonly written either with or without a hyphen. For example, use "pretrial" rather than "pre-trial." We will, however, continue to use hyphens in the words "co-defendant" and "co-conspirator."

7.   Do not use "Mr." or "Ms." unless necessary for clarity. In particular, there is no need to refer to a crime victim as "Mr. Smith" or "Ms. Smith" rather than "Smith." When it is necessary to use a title for clarity and the reference is to a woman, use "Ms." unless there is some reason to be more specific; *e.g.*, to distinguish a mother and daughter.

8.   Use the form, "petitioner was convicted *on* 17 counts of bank robbery," rather than "petitioner was convicted *of* 17 counts of bank robbery."

Note that, for example, when it states that "petitioner is convicted on one count of conspiracy to distribute methamphetamine, in violation of 21 U.S.C. 841 and 846," the paralegal needs to look to see when 21 U.S.C. 841 and 846 were *last amended* and when the *offense ended*. In this example, 21 U.S.C. 841 was amended in 2006, 2008, and 2010, while 21 U.S.C. 846 was last amended in 1988; and the offense ended on September 29, 2005. Here the sentence should read: "petitioner is convicted on one count of conspiracy to distribute methamphetamine, in violation of 21 U.S.C. 841 (2000 & Supp. V 2005) and 21 U.S.C. 846." It is the *attorney's preference* whether to make these edits.

9.   Use the form, "petitioner *pleaded* guilty," rather than "petitioner pled guilty."

10. Form the possessive of a noun ending in x or s by adding "'s" whenever that is the way it is pronounced. For example: Congress's, petitioner Jones's, and appendix's, but the court of appeals'.

E.   MISCELLANEOUS PUNCTUATION PREFERENCES

1.   There is no rule against having three consecutive parentheses. Although such punctuation is ugly and should be avoided, it is up to the author in the individual case.

F. MISCELLANEOUS TYPOGRAPHICAL PREFERENCES

1. In text that appears in a proportionally spaced font, a hair space should be used to keep a lower-case "f" or "j" from being too close to an apostrophe, quotation mark, parenthesis, or bracket. The hair space is after the "f," while the hair space is before the "j."

2. Bad breaks should be avoided. Examples of bad breaks include: *United* in United States per Webster's Dictionary as a geographical term; hyphenated words or hyphenated em dash phrases; S. Ct. should not be split; § or ¶ should not be split from its number.

3. Two spaces should follow a colon. However, attorneys have the preference of only using one space, but the brief must consistently follow that preference.

4. In IFPs, use "-- "; but in paid briefs use an em dash, "—."

5. For proper spacing, *e.g.*, F.2d or F.3d or C.F.R., make sure the "kerning for fonts" under advanced setting of font is *turned off*.

G. MISCELLANEOUS PREFERENCE

When making a global comment for an edit that appears repetitively throughout the brief, attorneys would like the paralegals to indicate that the global comment applies to that particular text by some notation.

APPENDIX

Response to FOIA Request for the Charles Fried Memorandum Referred to in Miscellaneous Grammar Preference 3

U.S. Department of Justice

Office of the Solicitor General

Executive Officer   *Washington, D.C. 20532*

JUL 2 5 2016

VIA U.S. MAIL or **VIA EMAIL to <22118-55760677@requests.muckrock.com>**
Brendan Kenny
MuckRock
DEPT MR 22118
P.O. Box 55819
Boston, MA 02205-5819

       Re: OSG FOIA No. 2016-125060

Dear Mr. Kenny:

       This letter responds to your Freedom of Information Act (FOIA) request to the Office of the Solicitor General (OSG), dated November 3, 2015, in which you requested records concerning "Memorandum from Solicitor General Charles Fried to Office of the Solicitor General attorneys dated October 2, 1987."

       Under the Freedom of Information Act, an individual is entitled to receive access to certain materials in identifiable agency records. OSG maintains primary pertinent records on current or recent past United States Supreme Court cases in which the federal government has participated. We also maintain records on adverse decisions submitted for the Solicitor General's decision regarding whether to seek further judicial review.

       Based on the information provided in your request, there were no pertinent records found in a search of our Automated Docket System. We searched our electronic repository of documents and found no responsive records.

       If you are not satisfied with the response to this request, you may administratively appeal by writing to the Director, Office of Information Policy (OIP), United States Department of Justice, Suite 11050, 1425 New York Avenue, NW, Washington, DC 20530-0001, or you may submit an appeal through OIP's FOIA online portal by creating an account on the following web site: https://foiaonline.regulations.gov/foia/action/public/home. Your appeal must be postmarked or electronically transmitted within 60 days of the date of my response to your request. If you submit your appeal by mail, both the letter and the envelope should be clearly marked "Freedom of Information Act Appeal."

                           Sincerely,

                           V. Yancey

VY/ss

www.ingramcontent.com/pod-product-compliance
Lightning Source LLC
Chambersburg PA
CBHW070043100426
42740CB00013B/2782